FIRST
PEOPLES
of NORTH
AMERICA

THE PEOPLE AND CULTURE OF THE
SIOUX

CASSIE M. LAWTON
RAYMOND BIAL

Cavendish
Square

New York

Published in 2017 by Cavendish Square Publishing, LLC
243 5th Avenue, Suite 136, New York, NY 10016

Copyright © 2017 by Cavendish Square Publishing, LLC

First Edition

Library of Congress Cataloging-in-Publication Data

Names: Lawton, Cassie M., author. | Bial, Raymond, author.
Title: The people and culture of the Sioux / Cassie M. Lawton and Raymond Bial.
Description: New York : Cavendish Square Publishing, [2016] | Series: First peoples of North America | Includes bibliographical references and index.| Description based on print version record and CIP data provided by publisher; resource not viewed. Identifiers: LCCN 2015045755 (print) | LCCN 2015045364 (ebook) | ISBN 9781502618955 (ebook) | ISBN 9781502618948 (library bound) Subjects: LCSH: Dakota Indians--History--Juvenile literature. | Sioux Nation--History--Juvenile literature. Classification: LCC E99.D1 (print) | LCC E99.D1 L34 2016 (ebook) | DDC 978.004/975243--dc23 LC record available at http://lccn.loc.gov/2015045755

Editorial Director: David McNamara
Editor: Kristen Susienka
Copy Editor: Rebecca Rohan
Art Director: Jeffrey Talbot
Designer: Amy Greenan
Production Assistant: Karol Szymczuk
Photo Research: J8 Media

ACKNOWLEDGMENTS

This book would not have been possible without the generous help of many individuals and organizations that have dedicated themselves to honoring the customs of the Sioux. We would like to thank in particular Cavendish Square Publishing for publishing this book and all who contributed to finding photos and other materials for publication. Finally, we would like to thank our families and friends for their encouragement and support along our writing journey.

CONTENTS

Killing the Bison • Reservations and the Ghost Dance •
Following the Wars

The American Indian Movement • The Black Hills •
Preserving the Language • The Sioux Today

Black Elk • Gertrude Bonnin • Elizabeth Cook-Lynn
• Crazy Horse • Ella Deloria • Vine Deloria Jr. • Little
Crow • Russell Means • Red Cloud • Sitting Bull

A Sioux man dresses in traditional clothing.

AUTHORS' NOTE

At the dawn of the twentieth century, Native Americans were thought to be a vanishing race. However, despite four hundred years of warfare, deprivation, and disease, Native Americans have persevered. Countless thousands have lost their lives, but over the course of this century and the last, the populations of Native tribes have grown tremendously. Even as America's First Peoples struggle to adapt to modern Western life, they have also kept the flame of their traditions alive—the languages, religions, stories, and the everyday ways of life. An exhilarating renaissance in Native American culture is now sweeping the continent from coast to coast.

The First Peoples of North America books depict the social and cultural life of the major nations, from the early history of Native peoples in North America to their present-day struggles for survival and dignity. Historical and contemporary photographs of traditional subjects, as well as period illustrations, are blended throughout each book so that readers may gain a sense of family life in a tipi, a hogan, or a longhouse.

No single book can comprehensively portray the intricate and varied lifeways of an entire tribe, or nation. We only hope that young people will come away with a deeper appreciation for the rich tapestry of Native American culture—both then and now—and a keen desire to learn more about these first Americans.

Many generations of Sioux lived in the Badlands of South Dakota, pictured here.

CHAPTER ONE

When I was a boy, the Sioux owned the world.

—Chief Sitting Bull

A CULTURE BEGINS

Like many other Native tribes in North America, the story of the Sioux begins thousands of years ago. Ancient ancestors came to the continent by way of the Bering Strait, which had created a natural land bridge between Asia and Alaska. Historians estimate this happened around ten thousand years ago. From there, these groups dispersed across the land. The Sioux's early ancestors came to live in the

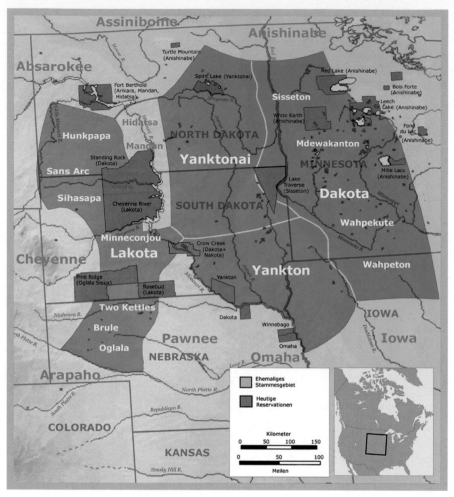

This map shows the territory of the Sioux Nation. Green represents Sioux land prior to living on reservations. The orange is the Sioux reservation land today.

southeastern United States. This area encompassed the present-day states of Florida, Georgia, North and South Carolina, and Virginia. They lived in this area until the 1500s, when they began to move northward, eventually settling in the midwestern state of Minnesota. However, some would relocate over time to areas as far west as the Great Plains. As years passed, they formed their own cultures, complete with their own beliefs, languages, and customs. By the nineteenth century, the Sioux would become a well-known name among incoming American settlers from the East.

The Sioux Begin

Prior to European arrival, the Sioux made their homes for hundreds of years in bark lodges among the forests and lakes of the north. They lived on game, such as deer, and wild rice, although in later years they also began to cultivate fields of corn. Men stalked deer, rabbits, and other small animals in the forest and netted fish in the glistening streams. Women glided silently in canoes over lakes, bending over the long grasses and shaking wild rice into their baskets. In the spring, they tapped maple trees for their clear sap, which was cooked down to sweet syrup. When game became scarce, they moved to another part of this country of woods and lakes, using dogs to pull small sleds called **travois** (trav OY). Occasionally, they killed a bison (also called buffalo)—at that time the large, shaggy beasts roamed as far east as the Appalachian Mountains. Gradually, the Sioux began to realize that the bison could provide nearly all their basic needs for food, clothing, and shelter.

Divisions

There were seven tribes of the Sioux people: Mdewakanton, Wahpeton, Wahpekute, Teton, Sisseton, Yankton, and Yanktonai. These original tribes joined in an alliance called the Oceti Sakowin, or Seven Council Fires. Every summer, they came together to talk and perform a **Sun Dance**. The council of forty-four chiefs discussed future plans for the nation. Four men from among the forty-four were chosen as great chiefs. These chiefs could not inherit their positions; only those who had proven themselves to be exceptionally strong, brave, and wise were considered. At the summer gathering, people also renewed friendships, shared news, and traded articles they had made or acquired from other tribes.

The Teton, from the word *tetonwan* meaning "Dwellers of the Prairie," were the largest of the seven groups of Sioux, with seven divisions of its own: Brulé, Oglala, Two Kettles, Miniconjou, No Bows, Hunkpapa, and Sihasapa. The Sioux received their popular name from the Ojibwa, who called the Iroquois, their powerful enemy to the east, "true snakes" and the Sioux to the west "lesser snakes," or *nadouessioux*. The French garbled the word "Sioux," a name that is now used for all the Sioux people.

The Sioux may also be divided into three language groups: **Dakota**, **Lakota**, and Nakota. Each of these names mean "ally" or "friend." A **sedentary** and agricultural tribe, the Dakotas were known as the Santee or Eastern Sioux, and the Nakotas as the Yankton and Yanktonai or Middle Sioux. The Lakotas were also known as the Teton, the Plains, or Western Sioux.

Warring Nations

For years, the Sioux battled the Ojibwa and the Cree in the northern woods. However, this changed when French traders arrived in North America. They began to supply the Sioux's enemies with muskets, or "firesticks," Sioux warriors were suddenly at a tremendous disadvantage. At the same time, they were impressed

The Sioux had great war chiefs and warriors. Here, Sioux chief Red Cloud (*seated, second to the left*) poses with his warriors, circa 1865–1880.

by the huge bison herds that roamed the prairies to the west. In the 1600s, they migrated once again—to the Great Plains of the Dakotas. The Teton were the first to transform themselves into skilled horsemen and bison hunters. They fiercely battled other tribes and eventually drove them from the plains.

By 1750, with thirty thousand people, the Teton had firmly established themselves in the heart of the northern Great Plains. Most of the Sioux living in the Dakotas today are descended from these Teton. Toward the end of the 1600s, the Nakota also moved onto the broad plains, splitting into the Yankton and Yanktonai branches.

The Santee remained in permanent bark homes in the woodlands. In later years, after the Minnesota Sioux Uprising in 1862, some scattered into the Dakotas, Montana, and Nebraska, although most Santee still live on a small **reservation** in their Minnesota home.

By the early 1800s, the Sioux had come to dominate the Great Plains. Excellent horsemen, they were admired as the "finest light cavalry in the world." Flying across the prairie, swift as the wind on their fine horses, the eagle feathers of their **warbonnets** streaming after them, they struck fear into the hearts of their enemies. With their sleek horses, they could hunt down enough bison in a single day to feed their families for months, leaving war parties of young braves free to sweep across the Great Plains.

The Barren Land

A wandering people, the Sioux have known many places—from the forests of the Southeast to the land of ten thousand lakes in Minnesota. Yet, for hundreds of years, most of the Sioux lived on vast stretches of the northern prairie—broad, rolling grasslands that flow like waves on the open sea in the unrelenting wind. Much of this landscape is interrupted only by an occasional streambed, a silver vein of water trickling through the ragged V of a ravine. In some places, the land is so flat that it appears to be the floor of the sky.

Early explorers described this land as the Great American Desert, fit only for "wild savages and Indian cattle," which is what they called buffaloes. Millions of the snorting beasts spread over the plains like a deep chocolate-brown blanket as far as one could see. This

According to the Sioux, the Badlands were places where ghosts and monsters lurked.

vast, open country, with neither a tree nor cabin in sight, gave the Sioux an exhilarating sense of space and freedom. Spreading far and wide, the plains were laced with several broad rivers—the Missouri, Platte, Cheyenne, Niobrara, and White. The riverbanks were fringed with stands of the sacred cottonwood trees, which became tattered ribbons of yellow during the autumn months. The Sioux often camped near these clear-flowing waters for protection against enemies and the elements. Otherwise, Sioux country was marked in each direction by the four winds, an overwhelming sky, and not a single other obstruction. It was a country made for great horsemen. Here, a warrior could ride for miles, day after day, with nothing to hinder him.

The land was also noted for its extreme weather—hot, humid summers and brutal winters. Intense winds roared down from the Arctic, bringing heavy snows and bone-chilling cold. Here, one could get lost in a blizzard, completely blinded by the swirling wall of white, and freeze to death in minutes. Yet the northern plains also knew the tender green of spring, the radiance of summer, and the golden light of autumn. Much of one's time during this joyous warmth was spent getting ready for the next bitterly cold winter.

Much was sacred about this land. Among the luxuriant grasses, the prairie was fragrant with the scent of sage and other herbs used by medicine men in healing rituals. Within the broad prairies were two extraordinary landscapes, one haunted and the other holy—the Badlands and the Black Hills. The Badlands was a place of fantastic, contorted rock sculptures. Most of the colors had been leached from the land by the occasional rains, until it was buff or pale gray, resembling the surface of the moon. It was a strange, mystical place, strewn with the fossil bones of dinosaurs and other ancient creatures. The Sioux believed that ghosts and monsters existed in the Badlands. They stayed away from this eroded place.

In higher country, the treeless prairie gave way to sweet meadows enveloped by craggy hills studded with dark pines. There were also clear lakes bordered with spruce and ponderosa pine, as well as juniper and quaking aspen. A sacred place to the Sioux, the **Paha Sapa**, or Black Hills, rose suddenly from the prairie—cool, shadowy, and mysterious. Many rocky landmarks, including the Needles and the Cathedral Spires, thrust upward in the heart of this magical country. Sioux elders told children that the Black Hills were the home of Wakinyan, the legendary Thunderbird, whose eyes were bolts of lightning.

Wild animals also made their home in this rugged country. Out on the prairie, birds tended nests hidden carefully on the ground, and the resourceful coyote, always keeping his distance, trotted along the margins of the human world. There were whole towns of prairie dogs, the rodents popping up then diving down into their burrows, and there were waves of buffalo. There were also swift, graceful pronghorn antelope springing away as quick and silent as the light. Roaming the Black Hills were elk, moose, mountain sheep, mule deer, bobcats, mountain lions, wolves, brown bears, and grizzlies. If a warrior was brave enough to face the ferocious grizzly with spear and bow, he could proudly wear a bear claw necklace.

Eagles and other birds of prey were messengers of the Great Spirit of the Sioux.

Overhead circled vultures, hawks, and eagles, the messengers of the Great Spirit in this wild, dramatic land. All the four-leggeds, as the animals were known, and all the winged ones were relatives of the two-leggeds, or humans. Every Sioux prayer ended with the words *Mitakuye oyasin*, which means "And all my relations." These relatives included not only people but all living plants and animals, from the smallest insect and the most fragile flower to the sacred bison, all of whom were warmed by the same sun and bound together as one in the universe. As expressed in a prayer by the Oglala Sioux holy man Black Elk: "Grandfather, Great Spirit, once more behold me on earth and learn to hear my feeble voice. You lived first, and you are older than all need, older than all prayer. All things belong to you—the

The People and Culture of the Sioux

two-legged, the four-legged, the wings of the air, and all green things that live."

The Stories of the Sioux

Deeply spiritual, the Sioux viewed themselves as a very small part of a vast universe that reached across the broad prairies to the very edges of the panoramic sky. The sun, the sky, the earth, and the four winds were central to their beliefs, as were the stars—the holy breath of the supernatural.

The Sioux also understood the realities of hardship, having faced cold and hunger and the uncertainty of nature. This direct experience, especially with death in battles and bitter winters, helped to foster their deep beliefs. These beliefs are vividly expressed in stories about their origins. Some stories recount their beginnings in the sacred Black Hills of South Dakota. Others trace the Sioux migration from the forests of Minnesota to the windblown plains. Based on ancient oral narratives, the following is a condensed story about how the Sioux came to the earth:

> Long ago, Waziya, the Old Man, lived beneath the earth with his wife, Wakanka. They had a daughter named Ite, who grew to be the most beautiful of women. She was so lovely that she caught the eye of one of the gods, Tate, the Wind. Although she was not a goddess, Ite married Tate, who lived at the entrance of the Spirit Trail. Over time, she bore quadruplets, all boys, who became the North, West, East, and South Winds.

Because his daughter Ite was married to Tate, Waziya was able to mix with the good and helpful gods. However, he yearned to have the power of a true god. Iktomi, the Trickster, who loved to spread discontent, promised Waziya, Wakanka, and Ite enormous power and even greater beauty for Ite if they would help him make others look ridiculous. He even promised Ite that her beauty would rival that of the goddess Hanwi, the Moon, who was married to the god Wi, the Sun.

The three of them agreed and Iktomi gave Ite a charm, which made her so beautiful that she was less attentive to her four sons. Wi was captivated by her and invited her to sit beside him at the feast of the gods. Ite arrived early and took the vacant seat next to Wi. When Hanwi arrived, she saw that her seat had been taken and she was so ashamed that she covered her face with a dark robe to hide from the laughing people—and devious Iktomi, who outlaughed everyone.

After the feast, the god Skan, the Sky and judge of all the gods, called a council to expose Wi, who had forsaken his wife; Ite, who dared assume the place of a goddess; Waziya and Wakanka, who had vainly wished to be gods; and Iktomi, who had deceived everyone. As punishment, Wi was to lose the comfort of his wife, Hanwi—he was to rule during the day

The Sioux made many objects from animals and plants around them, such as this painted bison hide, circa 1830.

A Culture Begins

and she would dominate the skies at night. Whenever they came out together, Hanwi would cover her face in shame. Because of her vanity and the neglect of her sons, Ite's next child would be born early and be unlike her other children. Her children were to live with their father, Tate, and she was told to return to the world and live without friends. Half of Ite remained stunningly beautiful, but the other half became so ugly that people were frightened by the sight of her. She became known as Anung-Ite, the Double-Faced Woman.

Waziya and Wakanka were banished to the edge of the world until they learned to help young children. Renamed for their misdeeds, they became known as the Wizard and the Witch. Iktomi was also sent to the edge of the world, where he was to be forever without friends. Tate, who was punished for marrying Ite, was told to raise his children properly and to do woman's work. He lived with his four sons, the Winds, and his fifth son, little Yumni, the Whirlwind, beyond the pines in the land of the ghosts. Each day, his sons traveled the earth, swirling in the four directions, according to his instructions.

In the beginning, the Wizard and the Witch, along with Anung-Ite and Iktomi, were the only people on Earth. Iktomi grew tired of playing tricks on the animals because they never showed any shame over their misfortunes, so he asked Anung-Ite what she most desired. After he swore to abandon tricks and pranks, she told him that she wanted people to come to Earth. She reasoned that if they tasted meat and learned how to make clothes and tipis, they would live where they could have these good things. Iktomi then went to the wolves, again promising to give up his tricks. So, they drove moose, deer, and bears to Anung-Ite's tipi, where she made food, clothing, and shelter to entice the Sioux people.

Iktomi gave a packet of delicious meat and fancy clothing to one of the wolves, which trotted through a cave out of the world and presented the bundle to a young warrior named Tokahe, the First One. When the other Sioux people tasted the food and saw the clothes worn by Tokahe, they were envious and asked how they might acquire such things. Led by the wolf, three men, along with Tokahe, entered the world through the cave to find the source of this bounty. They came to a lake where Anung-Ite had set up her tipi. She appeared to be a lovely young woman to Tokahe and his companions, and, posing as her husband, Iktomi seemed to be a handsome young man. The four young men saw much game, which Iktomi had arranged for the wolves to drive past them, and Anung-Ite gave them tasty foods and fine clothes to take back to their people. Iktomi also told them that he and his wife were really very old, but by consuming this earthly food they had remained young and beautiful.

Returning through the cave to their people, the four young men excitedly described what they had seen. Some people wished to accompany Tokahe, but others thought he was a wizard and doubted such wonders. The chief warned that anyone who ventured through the cave would never be able to come back. Six men and their wives and children joined Tokahe, and, guided by the wolf, they ventured onto the earth. It was not what they expected— they became lost, tired, and hungry.

The babies and small children cried. Anung-Ite appeared and tried to comfort them, but they saw the ugly side of her face and fled in terror. Iktomi then appeared and mocked the people who had been so foolish in coming to the earth. Tokahe was ashamed because he had urged these people to follow him. However, Anung-Ite's hideous face and Iktomi's deceit vanished when the Wizard and the Witch appeared. According to the prophecy, when they were banished to the edge of the earth, the Wizard and the Witch had learned to be tender and merciful to the young. They led the disheartened band to the land of the pines, to the world of the ghosts. They taught them to live as men and women. And this is how Tokahe and his Sioux followers came to be the first people to live on the earth.

The Sioux had many other stories discussing their origins and their beliefs. Over time, these tales were passed down from generation to generation. Today, many of these legends remain important beliefs for the Sioux tribes.

As years passed, the various tribes of the Sioux faced many challenges, but through it all, they persevered.

Black Elk was one of the Sioux holy men.

Every little thing is sent for something, and in that thing there should be happiness and the power to make happy.

—Black Elk, Oglala Sioux

BUILDING A CIVILIZATION

Early in their history, as the Sioux tribes settled into their everyday lives—largely in the plains—they established their own customs, traditions, and religious beliefs and practices.

Depending on the Bison and the Seasons

After the Sioux crossed the Missouri River, or Mni Shoshe (Big Muddy), they came to depend almost entirely on the bison that grazed the vast expanses of grassland. Moving with the bison herds, the Sioux hunted whenever they needed

Bison were essential to the Sioux way of life.

The People and Culture of the Sioux

food or materials for clothing and shelter. Living in cone-shaped tipis made from wooden poles and bison hides, they followed the cycle of the seasons or "moons." Each of these moons reflected a change in weather and activity.

The Moons of the Lakota

January	Moon of the Hard Winter
February	Moon of Popping Trees
March	Moon of Snow Blindness
April	Moon of Tender Grass
May	Moon of Green Leaves
June	Moon of June Berries
July	Moon of Red Cherries
August	Moon of Ripening
September	Moon of Colored Leaves
October	Moon of Falling Leaves
November	Moon of Starting Winter
December	Moon of Middle Winter

The Sioux spent the winter at the foot of the Black Hills, which offered shelter from the cold winds sweeping across the plains. April meant spring and the beginning of a new year. Men hunted deer, elk, bear, and antelope, as well as wild turkeys, prairie chickens, and rabbits, while the women gathered wild berries and fruit. Before moving out to the plains, they gave the bison time to fatten up from eating the tender green grasses.

A Way of Life

The Sioux formed themselves into groups, or bands, of family members called **tiyospayes**. Each band had

Men and women entered into marriage by living together. This picture is of a Sioux husband and wife.

one or more leaders of equal power, usually older men, chosen because of their wealth and wisdom. A chief had to be brave, honest, and intelligent, or he would be replaced by another warrior. In addition to keeping order in the village, these men decided when the group would move to another place, when they should go on a bison hunt, and where they would set up camp. They usually consulted medicine men to determine the best time for the hunt and then sent scouts ahead to locate the herds.

In addition to the older men who served as chiefs, young men who had proven themselves in battle became war leaders. No one had to join a war party, but if the leader had been successful, other warriors were usually eager to ride with him. None of the

The People and Culture of the Sioux

leaders had great authority. Living in small groups, the Sioux did not need an elaborate political organization. They relied primarily on public ridicule and gossip to punish those who broke the rules. Occasionally, a council of older men gathered to make a decision regarding a dispute, but they lacked the authority to enforce their ruling. Those men who had acquired guardian spirits during an adolescent rite called a **vision quest** also joined the Akichita, a kind of police force that kept order during bison hunts and relocations of the camp. Offenders were whipped with a rawhide lash, had their bows broken, or might even have their tipis and belongings destroyed. Most important, however, were a man's reputation as a hunter and warrior and a woman's merit as a mother and wife. Strength and skill were necessary to survive on the open plains, yet generosity was also revered in "giveaways." A man who owned many horses was honored, yet he was expected to share his food and belongings with the less fortunate members of the band.

Sioux families included not only children and parents but also grandparents and unmarried aunts and uncles. Grandmothers often helped with household chores and took care of the young children. Although men headed the household, children traced their heritage through both parents. The social order of the tiyospayes was based on male relatives—fathers, sons, and brothers. When a young man married, he usually remained with his father's band. This was partly because large groups of men had to cooperate in many dangerous tasks, notably hunting and warfare. The Sioux believed that men who had grown up together tended to get along better.

Tipis were made out of materials such as animal hides and poles, which could be taken down and transported if needed.

Rules of the Tipi

Good manners governed the tipi in which several families often made their homes. When people gathered around the fire for meals and conversation, the men always sat on bison rugs on the north side and the women on the south side. The head of the household held the place of honor within the circle at the back of the tipi, along with his willow backrest, pipe rack, and sacred things. It was considered impolite to walk between a person and the fire. Men, especially visitors, were always served meals first. Women and children had to wait until the warriors were finished.

The Sioux loved to get together with others, and bison humps or other tasty meats were always bubbling in the stew pot. The tipi was a good place to play the **moccasin** game, to sing sacred songs, to tell stories, or to boast of one's great deeds. Men loved to gamble

The People and Culture of the Sioux

and seldom undertook a contest that didn't involve a wager on its outcome. Everyone enjoyed guessing games. In the moccasin game, a pebble was placed under one of three soft leather shoes. Adults bet on which moccasin covered the pebble. Bragging was not only tolerated but encouraged among the Sioux, who needed to be strong and brave to hunt the bison, defeat their enemies, and endure the cold winters. Visits usually ended by smoking a pipe, which was passed solemnly from one person to another as the sweet fragrance of tobacco drifted through the tipi.

Making a Tipi

To make tipis, men traveled to the mountains to cut down long, slender pine trees to make the lodge poles. The strong, light poles were dried in the sun, then hauled to the village. To set up the frame, women tied three of the wooden poles together, raised one end of the bundle up, and spread out the bottom legs. They next placed eight or ten smaller poles around this frame.

Originally, the Sioux covered their lodges with bark, but when they moved onto the plains, they began to dress them with bison skins. To prepare the skins, women spread fresh hides on the ground and scraped away the fat and flesh with bone or antler blades. After the hides had dried, they scraped off the shaggy hair. After soaking the hides in water for several days, they vigorously rubbed in a mixture of animal fat, brains, and liver to soften the hides. They rinsed the hides and worked them back and forth over a rawhide thong to further soften them. Finally, the hides were smoked over a fire, which gave them a pleasing tan color.

Sioux chief Sitting Bull stands outside his tipi.

Several women cooperated in making a tipi covering. About fifteen tanned hides were laid out in a shape that would cover the tipi and stitched together. The hide covering was tied to a pole and raised, then wrapped around the cone-shaped frame and held together with wooden pins. Two wing-shaped flaps at the top were turned back to make a smoke hole that could be closed to keep out the rain. Always facing east to greet the rising sun, the U-shaped doorway was covered with a hide flap. Sometimes, women decorated the top of the doorway with porcupine quills, feathers, and horsetails stitched onto rawhide strips.

The design of the tipi allowed people to remain cool in the summer and relatively warm in the winter. During a heat wave, the bottom edges could be rolled up to allow the cooling breezes to flow over the inhabitants. During the winter, rocks and soil were shoved against the tipi to create a berm, or earthen wall, for greater insulation. Tipis also had a dew cloth made of bison hide hung on the inside walls from about shoulder height down to the damp ground. Decorated with paintings of battles, dreams, and visions, dew cloths not only kept out moisture but created pockets of insulating air. With a fire burning in the center of the earthen floor, the tipis stayed warm in the winter. According to an old Sioux saying, "A beautiful tipi is like a good mother. She hugs her children to her and protects them from heat and cold, snow and rain."

The tipi made a very practical home for the **nomadic** Sioux. Working together, several women could easily set up or take down a tipi in a few minutes. They used the tipi poles as a travois to carry the tipi covering and their other belongings. The poles were strapped to a horse or a large dog's shoulders and the other end dragged along the ground.

Important Animals

Originally, the only Sioux work animals were half-wild dogs—in fact, the dog was the only domesticated animal kept by any Native American tribe. The Sioux raised a large, powerful breed similar to the husky for carrying bundles and pulling travois. These dogs also kept watch at night. A smaller breed of dog was raised for food. Around 1750, the Sioux acquired their first horses from

The Sioux learned to use and value horses to travel the Great Plains and to trade with other Native tribes and settlers.

the Cheyenne, who had tamed the mustangs that had been roaming their land since the Spanish arrived in the 1500s. By the 1800s, millions of wild horses ranged throughout the American West, and the Sioux used horses rather than dogs as burden carriers.

The Sioux greatly admired horses, which could pull heavier loads than dogs and carry people swiftly across the plains. The Sioux had no word for these animals, so they called them *shunka wakan*, which means the "sacred dog." Men captured and broke, or tamed, wild horses, but preferred to acquire horses that had already been broken. Stealing horses from another tribe became a daring sport among the plains tribes. A successful raid brought status and war honors, and the size of a family's herd became a symbol of wealth. Generosity was among the highest virtues of the Sioux, and the giving of horses was especially respected. Horses also became a primary means of exchange—a man could trade horses for a wife or a rifle.

Frequently on the move, the Sioux no longer planted corn or made pottery. Why labor in the fields or stalk elusive game in the woods when men could jump on their horses and race after the bison herds? In a single hunt, they could provide enough meat to feed their families for months, as well as hides and bones for making tipis and tools. Household goods also had to be light and durable so they could be carried by a person, a dog, or a horse. The Sioux did not make pottery because it could be broken on their long journeys. Food, clothing, and other personal belongings were transported in leather pouches called parfleches (par-FLESH-es). Skins and other animal parts were used to store food and water.

Migrating

The entire village could be packed up to follow a herd of bison in a matter of minutes. The Sioux depended on the bison, in the belief that these animals gave their lives so the people could live. The band might stay in one place for a few weeks, if the herds continued to graze there, or trudge constantly along in pursuit of the thundering beasts. Usually they made camp near streams and woods. They needed water for cooking and drinking and trees for firewood. Constantly at war with the other plains tribes, the Sioux chose sites that could be defended against attack. They often had favorite camping places to which they returned season after season.

They lived this way for many years, until the first Europeans arrived on their land and changed their way of life forever.

An Oglala Sioux mother carries her child in a cradleboard.

The land is our mother, the rivers our blood.

—Mary Brave Bird, Lakota member

LIFE IN THE SIOUX NATION

The various tribes of the Sioux had different beliefs and practices for every part of life. They celebrated births, commemorated deaths, and as youths, they played games to prepare for the future. Life in the Sioux Nation was not always easy, but it was a life built on tradition and pride, and in many ways, it was those practices that enabled the Sioux to persevere in hard times.

Family Life

Sioux life centered on extended families of children, parents, grandparents, and aunts and uncles. These large families were essential because many parents—both fathers and mothers—died in wars and hunting accidents and from disease and hardship. If children lost one or both of their parents, through either death or divorce, they remained secure because they had many relatives within the band to look after them.

In addition to close family ties, the Sioux had many rituals and traditions regarding the various stages of life.

Being Born

When a woman was about to give birth, she remained in her tipi with one or more older women who served as midwives. Men were not allowed in the tipi during or immediately after the delivery.

Upon the birth of a child, the umbilical cord was put into a beaded bag shaped like a turtle, since these shelled creatures enjoyed long lives. The magical bag was fastened to a **cradleboard**. An identical charm, without the umbilical cord, was placed outside, perhaps in a tree, to fool any evil spirits that might harm the baby.

The birth of a child was a joyous occasion. Within four days, a feast was held to name the newborn, usually after its oldest living grandparent. As children grew up, they would receive additional names based on their character traits.

Growing Up

Parents did not have more children than they could care for. Often, they waited until a child was five or six years

This illustration shows Sioux women wearing cradleboards. The cradleboard with black feathers in it hanging above them is a mourning cradleboard.

old before having another baby, and they usually had four or five children altogether. Parents looked upon their children as their most precious gift. Children were never beaten and rarely punished; they were taught to be generous with others and to respect their elders. From an early age, they were also treated as adults and allowed to make their own decisions. Parents encouraged their children to follow the example of the men who had become the best hunters and warriors, and the women who had become most accomplished in providing food, clothing, and shelter.

Children grew up with aunts, uncles, grandparents, and other family members fussing over them and gently encouraging them to follow time-honored beliefs handed down through the generations. The grandparents, other family members, and friends of the family often served as a second set of parents.

Boys usually identified strongly with their father and his family. They were given small bows and arrows to practice shooting at toy bison. Playing with handmade dolls and toy tipis, girls remained close to their mother and her family.

Children were allowed great freedom, and the whole outdoors became their playground. During the summer, girls and boys played in the water and became fine swimmers. They played rough-and-tumble games of running, jumping, and fighting intended to build strength and endurance—traits needed to survive a rugged life as nomadic hunters and warriors. They raced each other on foot and on horseback. Boys formed balls of mud on sticks and flung the mud at each other until the loser was completely covered. In a game called "shooting the buffalo," boys practiced hunting skills by shooting an arrow through a hoop rolled across the prairie grass.

Three Sioux boys wear their traditional tribal clothing, circa 1901.

After the bison hunt, when their families settled for the winter along wooded streams, the children played "throwing it in," a game in which they spun a top over the ice. They sledded on curved bison ribs and slid across the ice on stiff bison hides. During these cold months, they also enjoyed stories told by their grandfathers. These stories recounted the adventures of the trickster Iktomi or recalled heroic deeds during battle or on a bison hunt. Children learned the history and customs of their people by listening to these legends.

Like other Native Americans, the Sioux did not have a written language; their history was passed down through a rich oral tradition. To help the storytellers remember, old wise men kept the "winter count," picture writing on tanned bison hides that recalled the key event of that year. For example, a "winter when the people died of smallpox" was represented by a face with red dots. Some of these winter counts represent more than two hundred years of history.

Coming-of-Age

As he approached manhood, a young boy went on a vision quest. This spiritual journey began with purification in a **sweat lodge** under the guidance of a medicine man. The boy was then taken to a hilltop where he remained alone for four days and nights to "cry for a dream." Some families dug special vision pits in the hillside. Here, the boy huddled and gazed into the sky for enlightenment.

Sometimes, relatives made a flesh offering for the boy. They cut small pieces of skin from their arms, placed them in a gourd, and gave them to the boy. They believed that the boy would be strengthened by the knowledge that dear friends and relatives had undergone pain for his sake.

Fasting alone, enduring the hot sun or pelting rain during the day, and listening to the howl of wolves at night, the boy hoped to receive a vision that would

The People and Culture of the Sioux

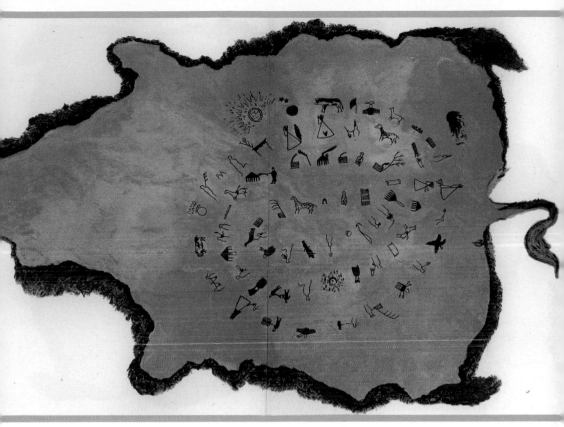

This is a winter count from the nineteenth century.

guide him in life. After four days, the medicine man brought him back home and interpreted his dreams for him. Men and sometimes women went on vision quests many times during their lives, but the first "crying for a dream" was the defining time of a boy's life.

At the onset of her first menstrual cycle, a girl also underwent a time of seeking to know herself. An old woman stayed with her for four days while the girl prayed and did her chores. The old woman then took her to the medicine man, who interpreted her dreams, after which the old woman bathed and dressed the girl in new clothes. Two or three weeks later, a feast was held for the girl. At this celebration, people danced and sang to honor her becoming a woman.

Marrying

Until about 1750, Sioux marriages were often arranged by the parents. Gradually, this custom gave way to young men and women choosing their own partners. A man usually tried to win honors in battle and hunting and acquire many horses before courting a young woman. Visiting her tipi, he sometimes played songs for her on a flute. If he thought she liked him, he would offer one or more horses as a gift to her parents.

Since many warriors lost their lives in battle, it was not uncommon for a man to have two or more wives, especially if he was a man of wealth and standing. This meant that more women were assured of having a husband and more children were born in the band. Usually sisters, these wives shared housekeeping chores, and their husband had to be able to supply enough meat for his family.

Marriage was an agreement to live together, with no vows spoken, and with an exchange of gifts between the families. Women were encouraged to marry and bear children. Virtue was expected of both men and women. If a woman was unfaithful to her husband, her punishment might be disfigurement by having her nose cut off. Marriage was meant to last a lifetime, but divorces did occur. If a couple did not get along, the wife simply placed her husband's belongings outside the tipi. A man who wanted a divorce announced that he had "thrown his wife away" and did not come home.

The People and Culture of the Sioux

Dying

When death came in battle or through old age, people were expected to face the moment with courage. However, after a person died, relatives entered a period of deep mourning.

The body of the deceased was placed in the branches of a tree or on a wooden platform called a burial scaffold. Personal belongings and offerings of food were tucked next to the body to comfort the soul. The favorite horse of the deceased was often killed so that its spirit might accompany the departed on its journey to the spiritual world.

Engaging in Warfare

Trusted allies of the Cheyenne, the Sioux were continually at war with the Pawnee, Crow, and other tribes that lived at the fringes of their hunting grounds. Warfare among the plains tribes was an exhilarating if dangerous experience. Many were killed or seriously wounded, and despite the honor of falling in battle, the primary goal was to come back alive.

After a victory, a war chief was humbled if he lost even one man. For young warriors, the main purpose of going into battle was "**counting coup**," which was as important as scalping dead enemies. Counting coup meant a warrior had gotten close enough to an enemy to touch him with a coup stick. Shooting an enemy from a distance was not as heroic or dangerous as riding or running up close enough to touch him. Small parties of young men eager to distinguish themselves in battle often joined an experienced leader "whose medicine was good" or who was known for his skill and luck.

These war parties made hit-and-run raids on enemy camps to steal horses, which were also a way of counting coup or avenging a relative who had been killed in a skirmish. These young men were usually members of one of the warrior societies, such as the Strong Hearts or the Kit Foxes. The highly renowned Kit Foxes wore a sash, which they staked to the ground during battle. This bold act meant the warrior intended to stand his ground until he defeated his enemies or was killed. The Kit Foxes sang:

I am a Fox.
I am supposed to die.
If there is anything difficult,
If there is anything dangerous,
That is mine to do.

The Sioux sometimes adopted captured enemies. During one battle, the great chief Sitting Bull encountered an eleven-year-old boy who courageously faced the warriors with his little bow and one last arrow. Sitting Bull shouted, "This boy is brave! I take him for my brother!"

Named Jumping Bull, the boy grew up to become a renowned Sioux warrior and Sitting Bull's best friend.

Hunting Bison

Using lances and arrows, men hunted bison in several ways. One man might track a single animal or small hunting parties might sweep down on several bison at once. In the late summer, large communal hunts—carefully planned undertakings—involved the entire band. At this time, men were not allowed to hunt alone and possibly trigger a stampede of the entire herd. Sometimes everyone in the band—men, women, and children—formed a V and stampeded a herd over a cliff or into a corral made of stones and brush. Another practice was to set a circle of small fires around the bison, which were afraid to cross the flames and smoke. The animals were then easily killed. Best known were the big hunts in which all the men in the band galloped after the bison, spearing or shooting the animals with arrows as their horses drew alongside them.

Boys took part in the big hunt soon after they learned to ride their spirited horses. Initially, they served as water boys and fire keepers while they learned how the men hunted the magnificent beasts. The killing of his first bison was a major, defining event in the life of a teenage boy. Afterward, his father held a feast in his honor and the boy received many gifts. He might also receive a new name to acknowledge his courageous deed.

Preparing the Bison

After the bison hunt, the women came to prepare the carcasses, and people enjoyed plenty of fresh

The Sioux relied on the bison as a source of food, clothing, and shelter. This painting shows Native Americans on a bison hunt.

meat. The liver and other organs that spoiled quickly in the summer heat, as well as the delicious tongue, hump meat, and ribs, were cooked and eaten right away. The majority of the fresh meat was packed on travois and hauled to camp. This red meat was thinly sliced and hung on poles in the sun. Smoke from fires burning beneath the wooden racks helped to keep the flies away and quicken the drying process. Women sometimes pounded the dried meat, called jerky, and mixed it with fat and berries to make **pemmican**, which men ate on long trips. However, most of the dried meat was stored for the lean months of winter. Everyone shared the meat—giving was very important to the

Sioux, especially to those who were the ablest hunters and warriors.

Aside from the bison meat, families made use of the horns, hides, and bones. No part of these revered animals was ever wasted. Men made tools—knives, scrapers, and needles—from the bones while the women turned hides into tipi covers, blankets, clothes, and moccasins. Rawhide was made into drums and war shields. Horns were fashioned into spoons, cups, and ladles.

Nearly two hundred different articles could be made from parts of the bison's body. Stretched over a frame, the hides became a makeshift boat for river crossings. The thick neck skin made good shields. Scraped to resemble white parchment, skins were folded into parfleches. The hooves were turned into rattles and even the tail made a good flyswatter. Rawhide strips were twisted into sturdy ropes and sinew was used as sewing thread. Bones were made into knives and scrapers, smoking pipes, and toys for the children. Most important, the painted skull became the altar for religious ceremonies.

Cooking Meals

In addition to making tipis, hardworking women undertook the arduous tasks of providing food for their families. Women gathered fruits, seeds, and berries, and dug wild potatoes and prairie turnips. Pemmican could be eaten without further preparation, but most meats, whether fresh or dried, had to be roasted over a fire or boiled. To boil food, women dug a pit in the ground, which they lined with animal skins and filled with water—or they used the lining of a bison stomach. The lining was stretched over the pit between four sticks and filled with water. Heated stones were then dropped into the makeshift pot for cooking meat and vegetables. Meals often included stew with wild turnips and bison meat.

Sioux Clothes

Women also made moccasins and clothing for their families from tanned deer or elk hides—knee-length dresses and leggings with buckskin fringes for themselves and sleeveless shirts, breechcloths, and leggings for the boys and men. To keep warm in winter, both genders wrapped themselves in bison robes. Often, the women decorated clothing and moccasins with porcupine quills that had been dyed many colors. The hollow quills were cut into similar lengths and sewn on like beads. Women embroidered moccasins with quills as a token of love for their husbands, sons, and brothers. Quilling required many hours of painstaking work, and women were admired for the quality of their artistry. When the Sioux began to exchange goods with European traders, they acquired glass beads, which quickly replaced **quillwork** as decorations.

Men used dyes to paint designs on their clothing. Some people painted or tattooed their bodies; children usually had their ears pierced when they were five or six years old. Both men and women wore necklaces and armbands of beads and bone, and both plaited their hair in two braids, weaving in colorful beads or cloth, although older women often wore their hair down. Some men shaved the sides of their head to make a

RECIPE

WOJAPI

This dish has long been a favorite dessert among the Sioux. Traditionally, this dish was made with pounded chokeberries, boysenberries, or blueberries. It is usually served with fry bread, but you can use pita bread cut into small wedges to dip into the fruit pudding.

INGREDIENTS

1 16-ounce (475-milliliter) can of blueberry pie filling
Cornstarch (enough to thicken)
Sugar to taste

Heat blueberry pie filling in a saucepan on the stove. Add a teaspoon (3.13 grams) or so of cornstarch to thicken the mixture as it heats. Sweeten the pudding with one or two teaspoons of sugar.

This doll was made by a Sioux grandmother for her grandchild. It wears a traditional Sioux woman's riding outfit.

"roach," or Mohawk-style haircut. Young men wore a single feather in their hair while older war leaders often donned warbonnets. Notches were clipped in the feathers to indicate the exact deed of the warrior—killed an enemy, killed an enemy and took his

The People and Culture of the Sioux

scalp, or cut an enemy's throat—as well as the number of coups the warrior had counted and the number of times he had been wounded in battle. Feathers were also used to decorate spears, quivers, shields, warbonnets, and pipes.

On special occasions, men sewed scalps into their clothing and wore headdresses adorned with many feathers, to show off their prowess as a warrior. In battle, they proudly wore their headdresses. Warriors had risked their lives to earn each of the feathers, which were symbols of honor—counting coup, stealing horses, or saving a person's life. They painted their faces and their horses with bright colors before going into battle to encourage the spirits to protect them.

The Sioux way of life was practiced for decades. Each of the tribes formed similar lifestyles and adopted the ways of a nomadic people. However, as centuries passed, some practices were phased out. Nevertheless, today many longstanding Sioux traditions remain part of the Sioux culture.

The eagle is sacred to the Sioux. This war shield includes the eagle on it to help channel the bird's power.

CHAPTER FOUR

From Wakan Tanka, the Great Spirit, there came a great unifying force that flowed in and through all things.

—Chief Luther Standing Bear

BELIEFS OF THE SIOUX

The Sioux developed an intricate belief system, most of which persists today. Despite hardship and the arrival of missionaries, who sought to convert the Sioux to Christianity, the Sioux culture and religious practices continued and became integral to many Sioux ceremonies.

The Sacred

To this day, the Sioux believe that many different kinds of spirits inhabit the supernatural world, all of whom are *wakan*, or sacred. **Wakan Tanka** (wah-KAHN tahnkah), the Great Spirit, or Great Mystery, includes all of these spirits, the most important of which are Wi, the sun; Skan, the sky; and Maka, the earth. The sun and sky are considered male, while the earth is female and the symbol of birth, nurturing, and growth. Other important spirits are the winds, the four directions, the bison, and the bear. As Flat-Iron, an Oglala Sioux chief, once said, "From Wakan Tanka, the Great Mystery, comes all power. It is from Wakan Tanka that the holy man has wisdom and the power to heal and make holy charms. Man knows that all healing plants are given by Wakan Tanka, therefore they are holy. So too is the buffalo holy, because it is the gift of Wakan Tanka."

The pipe is still the most sacred of Sioux objects. Representing the flesh and blood of the Sioux, the red stone bowl of the pipe is the head and the wooden stem is the spine, fitted together to make the whole person. There is no balance in the world without this harmonious

This sacred pipe was used by the Sioux in ceremonies.

The People and Culture of the Sioux

union of mind and body. The tobacco represents all living green plants. The smoke is the breath of the people rising in prayer to Wakan Tanka. The stem is decorated with porcupine quills, and the bowl is carved from red pipestone dug from a quarry in western Minnesota. The quarry is holy ground to Native peoples, where one may not raise a weapon. In the past, enemies dug peacefully together, and no one could be attacked as they journeyed to or from the quarry.

According to Sioux legend, the sacred pipe was brought to the people by White Buffalo Woman. Along with the pipe, she brought rituals to guide the people on the right way of life. After she had presented her gifts, she bid farewell, strode over a hill into the sunset, and changed into a white buffalo. Here is the story, adapted from a version told by Dakota chronicler Iron Shell, which recounts the origin of the pipe and the seven sacred ceremonies:

> And so it was, Whope, the daughter of Wi, the Sun, and Hanwi, the Moon, dressed in lovely clothes, appeared to two young scouts. So radiant was her countenance, so perfect was her figure, that the two men fell in love with her.
>
> As they beheld her, she spoke to them, "I am of the Buffalo People. I have been sent to this earth to talk with your people. Go to your leader and tell him to have a council tipi set up in the center of the village. The door of the tipi must face east. Spread sage at the place of honor. Behind the fireplace, soften a square of the earth and place a buffalo skull there with

a small rack behind it. I have matters of great consequence to share with your people. I shall come to the village at dawn."

As Whope spoke, one of the scouts was so struck by her charm that he approached her. There was a crash of thunder, and a cloud enveloped them both. As the cloud drifted away, the other scout beheld the lovely woman standing untouched, but at her feet lay the skeleton of the young warrior. She then directed the scout to carry her message to his people.

The scout returned to the camp and told the chief, Buffalo-Who-Walks-Standing-Upright, about his encounter with the woman. Preparations were made for welcoming this mysterious stranger according to her instructions. An escort of virtuous young men was chosen to lead her through the village to the tipi. By daybreak, a large group of people had gathered around the council tipi in anticipation of her arrival.

As the sun rose in the east, the beautiful woman appeared over the horizon. She carried a pipe stem in her right hand and a red pipe bowl in her left hand, which she joined together. In a stately manner, she walked through the village, entered the council tipi, circled to the left of the door, and sat down at the place of honor. When she was seated, the chief welcomed her.

Arising and holding the pipe, the woman told them that Wakan Tanka was pleased with the Sioux people, and that she, as a representative of the Buffalo People, was proud to be their sister. She told them that because they had preserved good against evil and harmony against conflict, the Sioux had been chosen to receive the pipe, which she held on behalf of all mankind. The pipe was to be the symbol of peace and was to be used as such between men and nations. Smoking the pipe was to be a bond of good faith, and a holy man smoking the pipe would be in communion with Wakan Tanka.

She addressed the women as her sisters, saying that in life they bore great difficulties and sorrow, but in their kindness they comforted others in time of trouble and grief. By giving birth to children, by clothing and feeding them, by being faithful as wives, they maintained their families. Wakan Tanka had planned it so, and he was with them in their times of sorrow. Next she spoke to the children as little brothers and sisters and told them to respect their parents who loved them and made sacrifices on their behalf.

To the men she spoke as a sister, telling them that all things upon which they depended came from the earth, the sky, and the four winds. The pipe was to be used to offer sacrifices and prayers to Wakan Tanka for all the blessings of life—and it was to be offered daily. She told them to be kind and loving to their women and children.

Whope told the chief it was his duty to honor the pipe, since through the pipe the nation lived. As a sacred object, the pipe was to be used in times of war, famine, sickness, or any other extreme need. She instructed Buffalo-Who-Walks-Standing-Upright in the proper use of the pipe, and she revealed the seven sacred ceremonies that the Sioux were to practice: purification, vision seeking, the Sun Dance, ball throwing, making a buffalo woman, making relatives, and owning a spirit. She stayed with the people for four days. Before leaving, she lit the pipe with a buffalo chip and offered it first to Skan, then to Maka, then to Four Winds. She smoked and passed the pipe to the leader. When he had smoked, she announced that her mission was completed, and laying the pipe against the rack, she left the tipi.

As she walked away from the village, fading into the distance, she became a White Buffalo Calf. In this way, Whope, the daughter of Wi and Hanwi, had returned to the earth to teach mankind. From that day forward, whenever a white buffalo appeared in a herd, no kills were made in that herd. The herd was sacred. And for more than ten generations the descendants of Buffalo-Who-Walks-Standing-Upright have cared for the sacred pipe on behalf of the Sioux people.

Today the pipe remains an important part of ceremonies and celebrations among the Sioux.

The Sioux had many chiefs and warriors. This is a photograph of Chief Bone Necklace, circa 1899.

Rituals and Dancing

Most Sioux boys were brought up to be warriors, but they could become holy men as well. These medicine men were honored for their ability to interpret dreams and visions. Among the most curious were the *heyokas*, who were also known as the thunder-dreamers, or forward-backward men. If a young man dreamed of the Thunderbird, thunder, or lightning, he had to act out his dream by becoming a heyoka. He had to do everything backward—say "good morning" in the evening and ride his horse backward—no matter how embarrassing. He became the sacred clown. But he also helped people interpret their dreams, which is how the Sioux believed messages were received from the spirits. Despite his supernatural powers, a heyoka led a very difficult, unhappy life. To be freed of this role, a heyoka plunged his bare arm into a kettle of boiling water and retrieved a chunk of meat. He was not burned, probably because his arm had been smeared with a special herbal salve.

Many religious ceremonies were held in the sweat lodge, a small, domed hut made by draping bison skins over bent willow branches. Inside the sweat lodge, people chanted songs, spoke their deepest thoughts, and prayed to Wakan Tanka. Four times the water was poured over the hot stones and four times the entrance flap was lifted, because, like the four winds and the four directions, this number was sacred. The pipe was passed from hand to hand, and the fragrance of the tobacco blended with the vapor within the lodge.

Sweat lodge rituals included purification when a boy embarked on a vision quest. An adult relative

A sweat lodge frame sits amidst barren land.

or medicine man usually guided the boy on his first "sweat." Participants huddled around a pit in the absolute dark of the sweat lodge. Outside, rocks were heated in a fire until they glowed red-hot. Then, they were carried on sticks, one by one, into the sweat lodge. As the medicine man prayed and poured water over the stones, the sweat lodge filled with hot steam—the sacred breath of Wakan Tanka. This steam cleansed the body and the soul. If the heat became too intense, the boy might cry out, "All my relations!" and the entrance flap was opened.

Among the important Sioux ceremonies was the *yuwipi.* Participants first cleared the tipi and laid out a sacred square with many small bundles of tobacco. They set up an altar consisting of a bison skull, a black and red staff, an eagle feather, and a deer tail. The floor was then strewn with sacred sage. Everyone had a twig of sage in their hair to receive the words from the spirits. In this ceremony, the medicine man, as interpreter between the spirits and the people, was rolled up in a blanket. The yuwipi took place in utter darkness. The only sounds were the rhythmic beat of the drum and a singer's chant, but soon eerie noises surfaced from the dark—high, birdlike, otherworldly. People heard the cry of the eagle and felt the touch of its wings on the walls. Tiny ghostly lights danced through the dark, and someone announced, "The spirits are here." At the end of the solemn ceremony, the yuwipi man was unwrapped and he explained the messages of the spirits who had visited them.

Uniting Tribes

Whether settled in winter camp or wandering the wide prairie, Sioux bands usually lived far away from each other. However, at midsummer, the bands gathered on the plains for the Sun Dance, the greatest of Sioux ceremonies. They arranged their tipis in a circle, leaving the center

The Sioux built their homes in all kinds of weather.

The People and Culture of the Sioux

open for visiting, ceremonies, songs, and games. Bands shared news about friends and enemies, as well as locations of the bison herds. Young people courted and old people gossiped at the large gathering. The men shared the sacred pipe and, with the rising smoke, sent promises upward to Wakan Tanka.

This hide painting illustrates the Sun Dance.

But the Sun Dance was the primary reason they had come together. This twelve-day event was a prayer to the sun and its warming rays, the source of life and renewal. It was also a sacrifice in which men showed courage and the ability to withstand excruciating pain. At the center of the dance circle stood the Sacred Pole, a forked cottonwood tree. Flags of the sacred colors of red, white, black, and yellow, which represented the four directions, fluttered from the pole.

The men wrapped red skirts around their waists and placed sage wreaths in their hair. Gazing at the sun and rhythmically blowing eagle bone whistles, they danced for four days. The skin of their chests was then pierced with sharp sticks tied to rawhide thongs and the Sacred Pole. At the end of the dance, the men had to tear themselves loose, the sticks ripping through their flesh. Women also pierced their wrists or collarbones. Sun Dancers underwent these ordeals to help unfortunate friends and relatives by assuming their pain.

Maintaining Traditions

The Sioux practiced these traditions for hundreds of years. However, in the 1800s, their lives began to change with the arrival of settlers. The presence of these newcomers, called "white men," would transform the plains into towns and cities, and would significantly reduce the land of the Sioux and other Native American tribes. Nevertheless, the Sioux beliefs persisted, even when the tribes were

The People and Culture of the Sioux

Today, the Sioux and other Native tribes still value horses for their beauty and aid.

challenged by different religious viewpoints. Today, the Sioux religion, language, and customs continue to be practiced by many tribe members, keeping alive the traditions of their ancestors.

The Sioux use many elaborate costumes to celebrate their culture.

CHAPTER FIVE

I have seen that in any great undertaking it is not enough for a man to depend simply upon himself.

—Lone Man,
Sioux member

OVERCOMING HARDSHIPS

Initially, the arrival of newcomers to the land of the Sioux was viewed as profitable by both sides. These new people—mostly trappers and traders—learned from the Sioux. They came to prefer life in the plains to life in big cities and wanted to make the most of their experiences. To do so, they established relationships with the Native Americans living there. Many early explorers, trappers, and traders learned Native American languages, adapted their styles of dress, and took up many of their traditions. Many also married Native women and lived with the tribe. In exchange for goods such as knives, rifles, gunpowder, coffee, and matches, the traders received glass beads, ribbons, furs, and hides.

For many years, the Native communities and these white men traded. However, there were consequences to the relationships formed. For example, traders introduced Native Americans to alcohol, which later had a devastating effect on these Native communities, as well as diseases such as smallpox and measles, which reduced Native populations. Over time, these relationships became more difficult to maintain, and as the French were driven out of territory by changes in government and war with British settlers, the Native people faced more difficult situations.

Sioux Relations Over Time

In the eighteenth and nineteenth centuries, relations between the Sioux and other Europeans became more challenged. The Sioux in the Midwest had worked with British colonials for many years, and during the American Revolution (1775–1783) and the War of 1812, the Sioux sided with the British. Once conflict between the British and the newly established United States settled, major changes for the Sioux took place. In 1815, the eastern tribes signed friendship treaties with the United States. Ten years later, another treaty acknowledged that Sioux territory included much of present-day Wisconsin, Minnesota, Iowa, Missouri, North and South Dakota, and Wyoming. However, in 1837, the Sioux were pressured into selling all their land east of the Mississippi River to the United States. Even

With the onset of railroads and other technologies, Sioux life was changed forever.

more land was sold in 1851 with the signing of the First Treaty of Fort Laramie.

Some of the biggest impacts on Sioux and other Native ways of life were American settlers and the advent of new technologies, such as railroads and telegraph lines. Throughout the early to mid 1800s, settlers moved in to Sioux territories throughout the Midwest and Great Plains. Before long, the US government built forts, cities, and towns to help the settlers. Newcomers did not show respect for the land and killed many of the bison, the lifeblood of the Sioux people. Furthermore, it became apparent that plains and West Coast settlers needed a way to travel and communicate more quickly with people on the East Coast. Railroads and telegraph lines were built, ushering in a new era of technology. As for the Sioux, eventually, many were forced on to reservations far from their Native lands. There, the Sioux endured terrible conditions and challenges. This had a detrimental effect on the men, women, and children forced to live there.

The Great Plains

Trouble on the Great Plains occurred largely as the result of settlers arriving in Sioux and other Native territory. Many of these settlers traveled in large groups called wagon trains. As they traveled, kicking up dust and hunting to supply themselves with fresh meat, they disturbed the great herds of bison upon which the Sioux depended. Then people began to **homestead** on the prairie, laying claim to land that the Sioux had hunted for generations. The Sioux did not like the stream of settlers or the forts the army was building deep in their home country.

Among the settlers was a young Mormon who had lost a lame cow on the range in the summer of 1854. A Sioux man killed and butchered the stray animal, after which the settler complained to Lieutenant John Grattan, the commander of Fort Laramie in Wyoming. The lieutenant wanted to make a name for himself and get promoted. He rode to the Sioux camp by the Platte River with twenty-nine soldiers and two **howitzers** and demanded the surrender of the warrior who had killed the cow. Refusing to hand him over, chief Conquering Bear agreed to pay for the cow, but Grattan rejected his offer. He ordered his men to fire, killing Conquering Bear. Angry warriors rushed from their tipis and killed Grattan and his troops. This sparked the Great Sioux Wars, which lasted thirty-seven years.

Homesteaders built on Sioux land and eventually set up towns and cities where the Sioux used to live.

The pattern of this war was one of raids and surprise attacks by the Sioux as they fiercely resisted the westward advance, and brutal retaliation by US soldiers. For the most part, the war was not fought in the plains tribe way of counting coup and winning eagle feathers. The soldiers zealously slaughtered women and children, as well as warriors. It became clear that the goal of the US government was not simply to win the war but to annihilate the Sioux people. In response, the Sioux caused havoc and brought terror to many settlers and soldiers.

Changing Times

In Minnesota, by 1862, the Santee (Eastern Sioux) were already living on reservations, but they were starving because they had no rations. They protested to the agent, or mediator between the government and the reservation, but he laughingly told them to eat grass. In what came to be known as the Minnesota Sioux Uprising of 1862, the Sioux revolted and many white men were killed, including several hundred settlers and soldiers. The cruel agent was the first to be shot dead. He was found with his mouth stuffed with grass. The uprising was put down, and thirty-eight Santee men were hanged in the largest mass execution in United States history.

Again and again, a truce would be declared and men on both sides would come together to sign a treaty. The Sioux always agreed to give up more of their land, and the Americans always promised that the Sioux would be allowed to live peacefully on their remaining land—and the treaties were always broken. In 1866, gold was discovered in Montana and in violation of the treaty, the Americans built a road through Sioux land. They also established forts to protect the prospectors along what came to be called the Bozeman Trail by the Americans and Thieves' Road by the Sioux.

In defense of their land, Red Cloud, a great Oglala Sioux chief, led three thousand warriors against Fort Phil Kearny in Wyoming. Captain William J. Fetterman, one of the leaders of the fort, was spoiling for a fight. One day the warriors attacked a company that had been sent out to cut firewood, and Captain Fetterman agreed to rescue the men. However, he and his men were ambushed and everyone, including Fetterman, was killed. This became known as the Fetterman Massacre.

Among the warriors was a young man who fought with distinction. He wore a magic pebble behind his ear and sprinkled sacred gopher dust on his horse to make him bulletproof. His name was Crazy Horse.

After the Fetterman Massacre, representatives negotiated another agreement with the Sioux, which became known as the Second Fort Laramie Treaty of 1868. The Sioux had to give up all the land west of the Missouri River and south of the Niobrara River. Again government officials assured the Sioux that neither white settlers nor gold seekers would be allowed on their land "as long as the sun shall shine and as long as the grass shall grow." However, that was not to be.

Custer's Last Stand

Another controversial figure soon galloped onto the scene. General George Armstrong Custer was known as the Boy General and the Glory Hunter, but the plains tribes simply called him Long Hair. Vain and ambitious, Custer surrounded himself with reporters. With one or two victories over the Native Americans, he expected to be nominated for the US presidency. In 1873, he led an expedition through the Black Hills and reported, "There is gold at the grass roots." Gold seekers swarmed over the Black Hills, digging into the sacred land, and the government did nothing to stop them. In fact, the government ordered all Native people, including the Sioux, to abandon their nomadic way of life, settle on reservations in Dakota territory, and "walk the white man's road." They set a deadline of January 1876, after which all Native Americans not on the reservations would be considered "hostile" and could be forcibly pursued, killed, or moved on to reservation land.

Since the Sioux did not travel much in the winter, many didn't receive word of the order and those who had simply ignored it. Open season was declared upon

This painting shows Custer's Last Stand.

the Sioux, who joined with the Cheyenne under the leadership of Sitting Bull, who had been a great Sioux warrior but now guided his people as a medicine man. Among the war chiefs were Gall, Rain-in-the-Face, and Crazy Horse. The army planned a three-pronged attack to kill or capture the "hostiles" under the leadership of Generals Crook, Terry, and Custer.

In June 1876, the Sioux and Cheyenne held their annual Sun Dance at Medicine Rocks in Montana. Sitting Bull offered sacrifices to the Great Spirit and received a vision in which he saw many soldiers falling down. He told his people: "We will have a great victory." Soon after the celebration, the Sioux were

The People and Culture of the Sioux

attacked by US soldiers. General Crook's troops first encountered the warriors, but after incurring losses and seeing the large number of warriors, he retreated.

On June 25, Custer approached the Native encampment near Greasy Creek. Scouts advised him that there were too many warriors, but the arrogant Custer believed that his Seventh Cavalry could defeat all the tribes of the Great Plains in a single battle. He was ordered to join General Terry at the Little Bighorn River on June 27, but rushed to engage the tribes the day before because he wanted all the glory for the anticipated victory. Dividing his troops into several companies, he attacked the village but was surprised to encounter so many warriors. Each of the companies was routed, and Custer retreated up a hill. "Brave hearts follow me!" Crazy Horse shouted as he led his warriors against Custer. In less than a quarter of an hour, Crazy Horse and his warriors killed Custer and his 225 men. Only a horse named Comanche survived the fierce battle. A young warrior named White Bull, Sitting Bull's nephew, most likely dealt the deathblow to Custer at the Little Bighorn. The fierce battle became the largest—and the last—victory for the plains tribes.

Killing the Bison

Bison hunters did as much as soldiers to destroy the Sioux way of life. "Send them powder and lead, and let them kill, skin, and sell until they have exterminated the buffalo," urged General Phil Sheridan. "Then your prairies will be covered by speckled cattle and the festive cowboy, who follows the hunter as a second forerunner of civilization." Soon the prairie winds carried the stench of rotting carcasses as hunters killed thousands of the huge beasts. "Where have all the buffalo gone?" the Sioux began to ask themselves, hoping the great herds would again come thundering over the horizon. But the bison had vanished, and the proud warriors were forced to surrender. If they did not, their women and children would have starved.

At one point, long before the first European and American settlers, there were an estimated sixty million bison living in the Great Plains. Once settlers arrived in large numbers and it became clear the bison offered many benefits—alive and dead—a great slaughter began. Not only were bison killed, but many were also captured and forced onto fenced land by private herders. In 1872, ten thousand bison hunters arrived in the plains. Every day of that year an estimated five thousand bison were killed. By 1884, there were less than two hundred living in the wild. Many Native communities suffered as a result of the bison being killed or relocated. A major part of their civilization was being eliminated from their lives, and there was nothing they could do to stop the damage. Over time, animal conservationists realized the destructive impact these mass bison killings had on the environment as well as the species. In the late 1800s, private herds owned by the government were established to help increase the numbers of bison living in the plains. Today, there is an average of four thousand bison living on their original grazing lands.

Reservations and the Ghost Dance

In addition to watching the bison population dwindle before their eyes, the free-spirited Sioux were shocked

by reservation life in which they were imprisoned within barbed-wire fences. Not only was their spirit ravaged, but they were cold, hungry, and sick. The government had promised rations, blankets, and tools, but dishonest officials frequently stole everything.

These were tragic days for the Sioux. "Friendly" Native Americans were turned against "hostiles," who wished to continue the old way of life. "One does not sell the land people walk on," Crazy Horse once said. He was jailed in a small cell but fought for his liberty. As Crazy Horse tried to break away, two or three men grabbed his arms, and a soldier stabbed him with a bayonet. His family placed Crazy Horse's body on his horse and fled to the hills, where they buried the great chief. To this day, no one knows the location of his grave.

Without their leader, cold and starving, the Sioux plunged into despair. Then they heard a message that, far to the south, a Paiute medicine man name Wovoka had died and come to life again. The spirits had given him a song and a dance that would bring all the slain warriors and the bison back to life. Wovoka's message became known as the **Ghost Dance** Religion, and it fired desperate hopes across the prairies:

Overcoming Hardships

A new nation is coming,
A new nation is coming,
The buffalo nation is coming.
We will live again,
Says the father,
Says the father.

Dancers whirled feverishly in the Ghost Dance until they went into a trance. When they awoke, they told of seeing the bison rising from a hole in the earth. They saw the white people's fences and buildings rolling up in a carpet, under which lay the prairie of their ancestors. The Ghost Dance was based on prayer, dance, and song—not violence. Yet, late in 1890, the agent at the Pine Ridge Reservation called for soldiers to put down the dance of lost hopes. Among the soldiers was the Seventh Cavalry, Custer's old regiment, which sought bloody vengeance against the Sioux.

On December 15, 1890, Native police surrounded Sitting Bull's home. They tried to arrest the great chief and holy man, but a gun battle broke out. Sitting Bull, his young son Crow Foot, several of his followers, and six police were killed in the ensuing outbreak. When word of Sitting Bull's death reached the Cheyenne River, the band of Ghost Dancers camping there under the leadership of Big Foot panicked. They fled toward Red Cloud, who was living at the Pine Ridge Reservation. They hoped the great chief, a friend of the whites, would protect them. However, a US army intercepted them 18 miles (29 kilometers) from Pine Ridge at a place called Wounded Knee.

Big Foot and his people surrendered peacefully and made camp, surrounded by several hundred soldiers, among them the Seventh Cavalry. The tribe made a powwow and socialized with the soldiers. The next morning, December 29, 1890, a shot rang out—no one knows if it came from a soldier or a tribe member, or if there really was a shot at all on that bitterly cold day. As the Sioux scrambled for their weapons, the soldiers fired upon the Sioux with their Hotchkiss cannons and repeating rifles. Women and children tried to hide in a nearby ravine, but they were hunted down and ruthlessly murdered by the soldiers. By the time the soldiers stopped firing their guns, they had killed nearly three hundred people, Big Foot among them. Afterward, the frozen bodies were stacked like firewood and buried in a mass grave.

The great Sioux holy man Black Elk, who was at Wounded Knee, later reflected: "When I look back now from this high hill of my old age, I can still see the butchered women and children lying heaped and scattered all along the crooked gulch as plain as when I saw them with eyes still young. And I can see that something else died there in that bloody mud … a people's dream died there … for the nation's hoop is broken and scattered. There is no center any longer and the sacred tree is dead."

This massacre, along with other history regarding many Native tribes in the West, was immortalized in the book *Bury My Heart at Wounded Knee*, written by Dee Brown and first published in 1970. This work changed the way many United States citizens and people around the world viewed Native American history.

Following the Wars

From 1890 to 1934, destitute and forgotten, the Sioux barely survived. Living on the edge of starvation, with poor health care, they had shorter lives than other Native Americans. The reservations had schools, a police force, and other buildings, but these services were of poor quality. Schools were inadequate—some had only three grades—and there were few jobs on or near the reservations. Many men, once great warriors, sank into the despair of drink. Sioux traditions and religious beliefs were discouraged or outlawed. Rituals took place in secret. Forbidden as "self-torture," the Sun Dance was performed in hidden, out-of-the-way places. There was no freedom of religion for the Sioux people.

However, after Franklin Roosevelt was elected president in 1933, he appointed two men who were sympathetic to the plight of Native Americans: Harold Ickes as secretary of the interior and John Collier as commissioner of Native American affairs. The Sioux were allowed to openly practice

Franklin D. Roosevelt made it legal for the Sioux and other tribes to practice their religions once more.

The People and Culture of the Sioux

their religion, and under the provisions of the Indian Reorganization Act of 1934, they were permitted to at least partly govern themselves. In addition to the tribal leadership, there was also a white superintendent on each reservation who exercised greater authority than the council. Major crimes were handled by the FBI and off-reservation courts—as they had been since their establishment—but tribal presidents and council members were popularly elected and tribal courts were established, along with tribal police forces. The Sioux gradually came to realize that they might once again have control over their own destinies.

As the years progressed, life for many Native Americans living on the reservations improved. Today, many tribes have **sovereignty** and are federally recognized as indigenous groups of the United States. Moreover, because of their efforts to preserve their history, many Sioux still follow the rituals their tribes have celebrated for centuries. They also continue to believe in the sacred circle, as eloquently expressed by Black Elk: "You have noticed that everything an Indian does is in a circle, and that is because the Power of the World always works in circles, and everything tries to be round … The Sky is round, and I have heard that the earth is round like a ball, and so are all the stars. The wind, in its greatest power, whirls. Birds make their nests in circles, for theirs is the same religion as ours."

A young Sioux boy wears traditional garb.

CHAPTER SIX

I see a time ... when all the colors of mankind will gather under the Sacred Tree of Life and the whole Earth will become one circle again.

—Crazy Horse

THE NATION'S PRESENCE NOW

Throughout their history, the Sioux have endured many hardships. However, they have survived them all, and today, they have continued their strong traditions and presence as an indigenous nation of North America. The twentieth and twenty-first centuries have brought many changes, successes, and difficulties to the Sioux people. Still they endure, and will do so for many centuries to come.

The American Indian Movement

In 1968, the American Indian Movement (AIM) was founded in the impoverished neighborhoods of St. Paul, Minnesota, because Native languages, religion, and traditions were being lost. Most of AIM's activist members were young urban Native people, including many Sioux. These young people began to visit Sioux medicine men in South Dakota to learn about their past. One of AIM's leaders was Russell Means, an Oglala Sioux from Pine Ridge, South Dakota. Crow Dog, a Brulé Sioux from Rosebud, South Dakota, became the medicine man for AIM. The Sioux also took a leading role in organizing the Trail of Broken Treaties, in which tribal representatives marched to the capital, Washington, DC, in 1972, occupied the Bureau of Indian Affairs building, and presented a number of demands for human rights.

The climax of the movement was the occupation of Wounded Knee, the same area of the battle against Big Foot, near the Pine Ridge Reservation in South Dakota, in February 1973. Several hundred people, mainly Sioux, protested the deplorable living conditions on reservations, especially at Pine Ridge. For seventy-one days, the protesters held off a heavily armed group of FBI agents, marshals, and Native police. Two Native people were killed during the siege, including Buddy Lamont, a Pine Ridge Sioux and ex-Marine, who was buried next to the Ghost Dancers of 1890. If nothing else, the protesters showed that they were proud to be warriors once again.

Since that time, Native American activists have become educators and founded schools to help

This photograph shows the dismal aftermath of the Battle of Wounded Knee.

children learn English as well as their own Native language. They have also run for tribal offices to help their people on the reservation. They have won lawsuits, including a $105 million payment for their removal from the Black Hills, granted in 1980. Still, many Sioux would still like to have the sacred land returned to them.

The Black Hills

Today, there is more activity concerning the return of Native lands to the Sioux. The Treaty of Fort Laramie in 1868, which stated the Sioux would not lose their ancestral lands, was quickly violated following the discovery of gold in Black Hills in the 1870s. In 1877, the government took even more land from the Sioux, including the Black Hills area. Since then, efforts have been made to reclaim original Sioux land, particularly in

President Barack Obama visited the Standing Rock Sioux Reservation in 2014.

the Black Hills of South Dakota. This is the most sacred area of the Sioux Nations; however, the Sioux are not in control of it. Many Sioux traditions and stories originate in the Black Hills area. The Sioux believe it is their right to control their ancestral lands. That would not mean people living there would be removed, however. Instead, a co-governance by Sioux and US governments would be enacted. As of 2015, efforts were being made to discuss plans of reclaiming this sacred land with President Barack Obama, who is an advocate for improving overall quality of life for Native peoples around the United States.

Preserving the Language

Over the years, many Sioux have worked to preserve their language and culture in a largely white society. Among the Sioux, there are three principal language groups: Dakota, Nakota, and Lakota. In the Dakota language there are four dialects: Assinoboin, Santee, Teton, and Yankton. Missionaries once zealously tried to destroy Sioux beliefs and language, but others have worked to preserve the Sioux language by preparing Lakota dictionaries and grammar textbooks.

Here are some examples of the Dakota language, which has been kept alive to the present day. The pronunciation key offers some understanding of how words are pronounced in the Dakota language. These examples are based primarily on *An English-Dakota Dictionary* by John P. Williamson and to an extent on *Everyday Lakota: An English-Sioux Dictionary for Beginners*, edited by Joseph A. Karol and Stephen L. Roxman.

Some Sioux words are nasalized, or spoken through the nose. These words are indicated by the "ñ." Here is the Dakota alphabet along with examples of the pronunciation. All of the vowels and consonants are spoken as in English, except for the following:

a	(ah) as in f*a*r
c	(che) as in *che*w
ç	a strong, exploded *c* not found in English
e	(e) as in th*e*y
g	(ghe) as in *gi*ve
g	a guttural sound, not in English
h	sound of *ch* as in German a*ch*
i	(ee) as in mach*i*ne
n	a nasalized sound, similar to i*n*k
o	(oh) as in g*o*
s	(she) as in *she*
t	an exploded *t*, not in English

u	(oo) as in *ooze*
z	as in *azure*

A few letters are followed by a break or brief pause indicated by '.

Here are some words spoken by the Sioux, some of which are especially important to them. Others are everyday words.

Dakota Terms

hoksidañ	boy
huñkawañzi	brother
tatañka	buffalo
hwksiyopa	child
wamnaheza	corn
suñ'ka	dog
maka	earth
atkuku	father
coñ'tañka	forest
koda	friend
wiciñyañna	girl
ti'pi	home
suñktañka	horse
huñ'ku	mother
hiya	no
tiñ'ta	prairie
piñspiñza	prairie dog
magazu	rain
wakpa	river
wayawapi	school
ta'winohtiñ	sister
mahpiyato	sky

añpetuwi	sun
mini	water
hañ	yes

A Sioux village on Pine Ridge Reservation, circa 1891.

Photo and copyright by Grabill, '91.
Deadwood, S. D.

The Sioux Today

The Sioux have not disappeared from the Great Plains.
Today, like their ancestors, female Sioux make lovely
beaded moccasins, purses, belts, and medallions.
They have brought back the tradition of quilling, using
naturally dyed porcupine quills for decoration instead

of beads. Boys learn to ride horses as soon as they begin to walk, and many grow up to herd cattle instead of hunting bison. Expert horsemen, many young Sioux work as ranch hands off the reservation and compete for prize money at local rodeos. Yet many Sioux still live in deep poverty. The tribes own several million acres of grazing land but lack the financial resources to build their own cattle business. Instead, many lease their land to white ranchers, who keep most of the profit. This is not the case for every person, however. A handful of Sioux now have their own small ranches.

Other issues face the tribes today, including high levels of unemployment, alcoholism, and mental illness. The Pine Ridge Reservation, for instance, has an unemployment rate of 80 percent, a high infant mortality rate, and a high rate of crime. Likewise, in recent years, the tribe has been shaken by a number of suicides among its young people. Mental health is an issue constantly being brought to the fore on reservations and other areas of the country. Many people struggle with the history of their people, oppression, and racism even today. Sometimes, these struggles manifest in depression or other mental illnesses. The Sioux have suffered, as have other Native tribes, but they have also endured. Difficulties remain and are being discussed by members of the nation and others in society.

In 2005, *National Geographic* photojournalist Aaron Huey spent time with the Lakota on the Pine Ridge Reservation. He dedicated the next eight years to documenting life there. His images were eventually published in *National Geographic* and his experiences compelled him to give a TEDxEd talk in 2010. He likewise wrote a book about his experiences, *Mitakuye Oyasin*, which was published in 2013. This experience was life changing for Huey, and he has since become an advocate for the Lakota and other Native communities.

While there are very real struggles for many Native people today, there are also successes. Many Sioux men and women attend college and have gradually assumed professional positions as teachers, nurses, doctors, lawyers, engineers, and reservation administrators. As a result, many people have moved from the reservations into larger, more urban communities. Even so, they do not forget their origins. A computer programmer, living in a modern house, may consult a medicine man as well as a modern doctor. A woman might attend a Christian church but also take part in a traditional ceremony. Her husband may purify himself in a sweat lodge ceremony.

Because of their generosity, many Sioux do not save money or manage their personal finances with care. To honor a dead relative, families still hold a giveaway feast in which they feed all comers and hand out many valuable gifts to the poor. Just as the hunter of the past donated a portion of his game to the helpless people—the elderly, the widows, and the orphans—the Sioux still share their income and food with the needy. This is an admirable philosophy, but it does not help their families if they give away so much that they are left impoverished themselves. As a result, many families struggle.

Powwows, or *wacipi*, have become a means of strengthening Native roots. Traditionally, the Sioux

Every year, the Sioux and other Native American tribes celebrate their heritage in powwows and ceremonies.

gathered in the spring to celebrate the seasonal renewal of life. People sang, danced, and prayed to Wakan Tanka. Today the powwow is central to the Sioux way of life. Throughout the year, various Sioux tribes offer powwows to celebrate many events. Annual powwows, such as the Oglala Nation Powwow and Rodeo on the Pine Ridge Reservation, likewise draw many visitors, as well as participants. For a full list of powwows in the South Dakota region, visit: www. travelsouthdakota.com/before-you-go/about-south-dakota/plains-indians/powwows-celebrations.

The People and Culture of the Sioux

Typically, the powwow begins with the grand entry, in which the eagle staff, along with the US, state, and tribal flags are carried into the circle. Invited dignitaries and all the participants then dance in a circle, clockwise. Accompanied by drum music and songs, the dancers perform in different categories: men's traditional dance, grass dance, and fancy dance; women's fancy dance, jingle dress dance, and intertribal dance. There are also honor songs and giveaways acknowledging the past when a chief would donate horses, food, blankets, and other possessions to the needy.

The Sioux population continues to grow steadily; today, there are over 112,100 Sioux in the United States. Most live on reservations in the Dakotas, as well as in Minnesota, Montana, and Nebraska.

Despite struggles, the Sioux have cause to be hopeful. They have committed themselves to keeping alive the language, beliefs, and traditions of their ancestors because "a people without history is like wind in the buffalo grass." Proud warriors and powerful women, they have endured the most outrageous abuse, including wholesale slaughter of their people. If they can survive such mistreatment, the Sioux believe they can once again prosper as a people. Just as the noble bison have come back to the windblown plains, so too the Sioux sing, "We shall live again. We shall live again."

The Sioux have many branches and many descendants. Because of this and their efforts to preserve their heritage, they are one of the largest Native American groups in the United States. Known for their bravery, their nation will continue to persevere.

Chief Sitting Bull,
circa 1880.

CHAPTER SEVEN

*With all things
and in all things,
we are relatives.*

—Sioux proverb

FACES OF THE SIOUX

During their long history, many Sioux men and women have made their name in the history of their tribe as well in the history of the early western United States. Here are some of the most well-known Sioux, from early times to the present.

Black Elk (1863–1950) was born on the Little Powder River in eastern Wyoming. At the age of five, he had his first vision; he had another when he was nine. He interpreted these visions to mean that he was to work to keep the Sioux religion alive. At thirteen, he took part in the Battle of Little Bighorn, after which his family joined Crazy Horse on his mission to preserve Native American lands and culture. Following Crazy Horse's death in 1877, his family went with Sitting Bull to Canada.

About this time, Black Elk was recognized as a holy man. He went with his family to the Pine Ridge Reservation, where he was often consulted for his visions. From 1886 to 1889, he toured the eastern United States and Europe with Buffalo Bill Cody's Wild West Show. At first he did not believe in the Ghost Dance. Yet gradually, his feelings changed. Tormented by the massacre at Wounded Knee, he became convinced that all people must live in harmony and that the new religion held an important message for the Sioux.

In 1930, Nebraska poet John G. Neihardt visited Black Elk at Pine Ridge and the next year recorded his oral history. The holy man's account was published in *Black Elk Speaks: Being The Life Story of a Holy Man of the Oglala Sioux*. Black Elk's wise and poetic words have since been widely published throughout the world.

Gertrude Bonnin (1876–1938) was born on the Yankton Sioux agency in South Dakota in the same year as the Battle of the Little Bighorn, to a Sioux mother and a European-American father. Although she distrusted most non-Native Americans, she sought an education against her mother's wishes. Attending the Boston

Conservatory of Music, she became an accomplished violinist. She later began to publish articles and poems in popular magazines and became known as a reformer who strove to expand opportunities for Native Americans and to safeguard their cultures. Her autobiographical book, *American Indian Stories* (1921) describes her changing views of the European-American world and her acceptance of Christianity. She also published *Old Indian Legends* (1901).

With Charles Eastman, she co-founded the Society of American Indians, which worked on behalf of Native Americans from 1911 to the mid-1920s. Bonnin also taught for a while at Carlisle Indian School in Pennsylvania. Under the pen name of Zitkala-sa, she investigated white settlers who had swindled the Indians of Oklahoma. An advisor to the Meriam Commission in the 1920s, she remained active in Native causes until her death.

Elizabeth Cook-Lynn (1930–) was born on the Crow Creek Reservation at Fort Thompson, South Dakota. Her grandfather was a Sioux linguist who helped to prepare early dictionaries of the Dakota language. Educated at South Dakota State College, the University of South Dakota, the University of Nebraska, and Stanford University, she became a highly regarded poet, editor, and professor. For many years, she co-founded and edited *Wicazo Sa Review*, a leading journal of Native American studies.

She has widely published in literary journals and anthologies. Her published works include *Then Badger Said This* (1978); *Seek the House of Relatives* (1983);

The Power of Horses & Other Stories (1990); *From the River's Edge* (1991); and *New Indians, Old Wars* (2007).

Crazy Horse (circa 1842–1877) was born on Rapid Creek not far from present-day Rapid City, South Dakota. His father was an Oglala medicine man and his mother was a Brulé who died when he was still young. Just before he turned twelve, Crazy Horse killed a bison and received his first horse. Around this time, he witnessed the brutality of American soldiers against Sioux people, after which he went on a vision quest. He dreamed of a rider in a storm, a great warrior with long unbraided hair and a zigzag lightning design on his cheek. Afterward, he received his father's name of Crazy Horse.

At age sixteen, Crazy Horse took part in his first battle—a raid against the Crow. He showed great courage and skill in the War of the Bozeman Trail of 1866–1868. He became war chief of the Oglala Sioux in 1868 and led attacks against railroad surveyors, gold prospectors, and soldiers for the next ten years. At the Battle of Little Bighorn, Crazy Horse led the attack on General George Armstrong Custer's troops from the north and west. Crazy Horse led his eight hundred warriors in other skirmishes, but exhausted and starving, he surrendered in 1877. His people never received the reservation promised them, and on September 5, 1877, a soldier killed Crazy Horse with a bayonet, supposedly for resisting arrest.

Ella Deloria (1888–1971) was born on the Yankton Sioux Reservation. Her father was an Episcopal minister of French descent, and her mother was a Yankton Sioux. She attended boarding school in Sioux Falls, South Dakota, and later Oberlin College and Columbia University. While attending Columbia, she worked with anthropologist Franz Boas in translating a number of Lakota stories. Over the years, she continued to work with Boas on traditional Lakota stories and Dakota grammar. Much of her work is unpublished, including "Dakota Autobiographies" and "Dakota Speeches," both of which were written in the late 1930s. Among her published works are *Waterlily*, a fictional study of her culture written in the 1940s but not published until 1988, and *Speaking of Indians* (1944), an essay about Sioux lifeways. In most of her writing, Deloria deals with the difficulty of relationships and cultural conflict between Native and European-American viewpoints.

Vine Deloria Jr. (1933–2005), a Standing Rock Sioux and the nephew of Ella Deloria, was born on the Pine Ridge Reservation in South Dakota. Educated at Iowa State University and the University of Colorado Law School, Deloria became a well-known public speaker on Native American issues. A highly regarded author, he has published *Custer Died for Your Sins* (1969); *We Talk You Listen: New Tribes, New Turf* (1970); *God Is Red* (1973); and *Red Earth, White Lies: Native Americans and the Myth of Scientific Fact* (1995).

In the 1980s, Deloria supported Sioux efforts to return the sacred Black Hills to his people. He served as executive director of the National Congress of American Indians and until 2000, he taught history at the University of Colorado's Center for the Study of Ethnicity and Race in America. He died in 2005 at the age of seventy-two.

Little Crow (ca. 1810–1863) became leader of his Sioux band when his father, who was chief, died in 1834. He maintained good relations with the whites who had settled near his home in present-day St. Paul, Minnesota. In 1851, he signed a treaty, giving up much of his people's land in exchange for a reservation on the upper Minnesota River. In 1857, he and his warriors attacked a renegade band of Wahpekute Sioux, and a year later he joined a Sioux treaty delegation that went to Washington, DC.

However, the Sioux became angry as more settlers moved into the region and threatened the Sioux way of life. At first, Little Crow sought peace, but then he assumed leadership in the Minnesota Sioux Uprising of 1862. Many settlers were killed or taken captive, but by year's end, the revolt was put down. More than three hundred people were sentenced to die on the gallows, but President Abraham Lincoln pardoned most of the men. Still, thirty-eight warriors were hanged, the largest mass execution in United States history.

Little Crow and his son escaped, but while picking berries, they were ambushed by settlers who wanted the $25 bounty on Sioux scalps. His son managed to get away, but Little Crow was murdered. Later, the Minnesota Historical Society put his skeleton and scalp on display, but eventually his remains were returned to the Sioux for proper burial.

Russell Means (1940–2012) was born in Porcupine, South Dakota, on the Pine Ridge Reservation and raised in Oakland, California. His mother was Yankton Sioux and his father was part Oglala and part Irish. In addition to a career as a public accountant, Means became a

Russell Means in 1974.

Native American dancer and rodeo rider before going to the Rosebud Reservation in South Dakota. After moving to Cleveland, Ohio, he became director of the Cleveland Indian Center and worked to transform the organization into a chapter of the American Indian Movement (AIM). Outspoken and charismatic, Means quickly emerged as one of AIM's principal leaders. In the early 1970s, he was involved in several protests, including the 1973 siege of Wounded Knee in which two Native people were killed.

From 1973 to 1980, Means was tried in four cases related to his political activities. Imprisoned for a year in South Dakota, he survived stabbings and shootings by inmates. He continued to take a leading role in political protests, including Yellow Thunder Camp, a settlement in the Black Hills. In the 1990s, he also began an acting career and appeared in several popular movies, including *The Last of the Mohicans* (1992), *Pocahontas* (1995), and *Buffalo Girls* (1995). He died in 2012 at the age of seventy-five.

Red Cloud (about 1822–1909) was born near the Platte River in present-day north-central Nebraska. Because of his bravery, he became chief of his band, and over his lifetime, he counted eighty coups. During the 1860s, prospectors traveled across bison hunting grounds on the Oregon Trail and a branch called the Bozeman Trail that led to eastern Montana. Red Cloud and his Oglala Sioux joined other Sioux and Cheyenne bands to attack wagon trains and military patrols on both trails. In 1866, Red Cloud rode into Fort Laramie to sign a peace treaty but left when the government would not agree to stop building forts on the Bozeman Trail. Two forts were completed and came under siege, culminating in 1866 in the Fetterman Massacre in which Captain Fetterman and eighty of his men were killed.

In the Fort Laramie Treaty of 1868, the government promised to abandon its posts along the Bozeman Trail and establish the Great Sioux Reservation, and Red Cloud and the other leaders agreed to cease their

raids on army forts and wagon trains. The Sioux celebrated by burning the forts soon after they were evacuated. Red Cloud traveled to Washington, DC, to meet with President Ulysses S. Grant and Ely Parker, the Seneca commissioner of Native American affairs. However, in 1874, General George Armstrong Custer violated the treaty by leading a mining expedition into the Black Hills, which led to a rush of miners and more conflict.

Despite the restless spirit of his warriors, Red Cloud advocated peace with the whites. After the victory at Little Bighorn, in which his son Jack and others in his band took part, government officials accused Red Cloud of aiding militant Sioux and relocated him to the Pine Ridge agency in 1878. He was deposed as chief of Pine Ridge in 1881. When the Ghost Dance swept the Great Plains, he still favored peace but was unable to control his warriors. Suffering from poor health in his later years, he died in 1909.

Sitting Bull (ca. 1831–1890) was born along the Grand River near present-day Bullhead, South Dakota. A Hunkpapa Sioux, as a young man, he proved himself a fine warrior and hunter, killing his first bison at age ten and counting his first coup against a Crow at age fourteen. Following his vision quest, he was accepted into the Strong Hearts, a warrior society of which he became chief at the age of twenty-two. During the 1850s, he distinguished himself in battle against other tribes but avoided confrontations with the whites who were coming into the region.

Following the Minnesota Sioux Uprising of 1862, Sitting Bull and his band attacked some of the army's scouting parties. During the War of the Bozeman Trail of 1866–1868 and the War for the Black Hills of 1876–1877, he and the Strong Hearts attacked small parties of settlers and prospectors. Around this time, Sitting Bull came to be recognized as a spiritual leader as well as a great warrior. In mid-June of 1876, Sitting Bull held a three-day Sun Dance in which he had a vision of soldiers falling dead. On June 17, the forces of Sitting Bull and Crazy Horse allied to defeat General Crook in the Battle of the Rosebud River. Just eight days later, the Sioux and Cheyenne defeated George Armstrong Custer at the Battle of the Little Bighorn. The victory, however, led to a stepped-up military campaign against the plains tribes. After a series of defeats, many of the Sioux surrendered, but Sitting Bull and some of his followers went to Canada.

When Canada refused to help him, he and his followers returned to the United States and surrendered in 1881. Held prisoner for two years, he was finally allowed to settle on the Standing Rock Reservation in North Dakota in 1883. For a year, during 1885–1886, he toured with Buffalo Bill Cody's Wild West Show

The Sioux look to the younger generation to continue their history, beliefs, and culture.

but was disgusted by the disrespectful audiences and returned to the reservation. Because of his opposition to the further breakup of the Sioux reservation and his resistance to white customs and policies, he came into conflict with Indian agent James McLaughlin. When Sitting Bull invited a group of Ghost Dancers to the reservation, the unscrupulous McLaughlin ordered his arrest. Sitting Bull was killed in a gun battle between Native police and his supporters. Because of this tragic incident, Big Foot and his band fled the reservation, which led to the Wounded Knee Massacre of 1890.

The people of the Sioux have a long history. Many men and women have made the tribe what it is today. Without them, the Sioux nation may cease to exist.

CHRONOLOGY

1500s Siouan tribes migrate from eastern North America and settle in what is now Minnesota.

mid-1600s Many Sioux begin to migrate to the Great Plains from present-day Minnesota.

mid-1700s The Sioux acquire horses and learn to use them expertly. Nomadic bison hunters, the Sioux dominate the other tribes of the Great Plains.

1800s The Great Sioux Nation dominates the northern plains, including the present-day Dakotas, northern Nebraska, eastern Wyoming, and southeastern Montana.

1803 The United States purchases the Louisiana Territory from France, a vast area that includes Sioux home country. In the following years, trading posts are established throughout the West.

1804 The Sioux encounter the Lewis and Clark expedition of 1803–1806.

circa 1831 Sitting Bull is born.

1837–1870 At least four smallpox epidemics ravage the tribes of the Great Plains.

circa 1842 Crazy Horse is born.

1849 The United States government purchases Fort Laramie from the American Fur Company and brings in troops.

1851 The Eastern Sioux are forced to sell their land in Minnesota and move to reservations. The first of the Fort Laramie treaties is signed with the Sioux and other tribes. Miners and wagon trains of settlers travel over what becomes known as the Bozeman Trail.

1854 The Sioux first encounter US military forces. John L. Grattan and US soldiers are wiped out at the North Platte River, thus beginning the Great Sioux Wars.

1855 Brulé chief Conquering Bear is killed in a dispute over a cow. His people avenge his death by killing thirty soldiers. In retaliation, Colonel William Harney leads 1,300 troops in a massacre of an entire Brulé village.

1862 The Homestead Act leads to a flood of settlers on Native lands. The Eastern Sioux fight back in the Great Sioux Minnesota Uprising of 1862. Following the revolt, thirty-eight Sioux men are executed.

1864 Colonel Chivington leads an attack against Black Kettle's camp in Colorado, slaughtering 105 Cheyenne women and children and 28 men, in what became known as the Sand Creek Massacre.

1865 General Patrick Connor organizes an invasion of the Powder River Basin, from the Black Hills to the Bighorn Mountains. They had a single order: "Attack and kill every male Indian over twelve years of age." In late autumn, nine treaties are signed with Sioux tribes.

1866 Young Sioux warriors, including Crazy Horse, ambush troops under the command of Captain Fetterman and kill eighty soldiers in the Fetterman Massacre, also known as the Battle of the Hundred Slain.

1866–1868 Chief Red Cloud leads a successful battle to close the Bozeman Trail, a trail to the gold mines of Montana that crossed Teton hunting grounds.

1868 The Great Sioux Reservation, encompassing most of South Dakota west of the Missouri River, is established. The United States promises to keep settlers out of this territory, including the Black Hills.

1874 The Sioux people defend their homes and way of life from a flood of prospectors seeking gold in the Black Hills.

1875 The United States government orders the Sioux to report to reservations by January 1876 or be declared "hostile."

1876 General Custer attacks Crazy Horse's large winter camp. In late June, Sitting Bull, Crazy Horse, Gall, and several Cheyenne leaders defeat Custer and the 7th Cavalry at the Battle of Little Bighorn.

1877 Sitting Bull escapes to Canada. Crazy Horse surrenders at Fort Robinson, and a small band of Miniconjou Sioux is defeated by General Nelson Miles. On September 6, Crazy Horse is killed. The United States takes over the Black Hills.

1881 Sitting Bull and 186 followers surrender at Fort Buford. He is imprisoned at Fort Randall for two years instead of being pardoned, as promised.

1887 The General Allotment Act reduces the land of Native American nations by giving 160 acres (65 hectares) to each family and 80 acres (32 ha) to individuals.

1889 An act of Congress divides the Great Sioux Reservation into six regions. Some tribes begin the Ghost Dance, a religious ceremony to restore their way of life on the plains. Late in the year, South Dakota is admitted into the Union.

1890 Sitting Bull is murdered on the Standing Rock Reservation, prompting Big Foot and his band to flee to Pine Ridge for protection under Red Cloud. Two hundred people in Big Foot's band are massacred by the Seventh Cavalry at Wounded Knee on December 29, thus ending the Great Sioux Wars.

1910 The United States government prohibits the Sun Dance of the plains tribes.

1924 The United States recognizes all Native Americans born within the states and territories as citizens.

1934 The Indian Reorganization Act recognizes tribal governments and provides financial assistance.

1973 Members of the American Indian Movement seize the village of Wounded Knee on the Pine Ridge Reservation.

1980 The United States Supreme Court orders the federal government to pay the Sioux tribes for land taken illegally.

1982 The Sioux lose a Supreme Court case to regain ownership of the Black Hills of South Dakota.

1990 South Dakota governor George S. Mickelson and

tribal representatives proclaim 1990, the hundred-year anniversary of Wounded Knee, as a Year of Reconciliation. A Century of Reconciliation is declared a year later, in 1991.

2005 *National Geographic* photographer Aaron Huey starts an eight-year-long project documenting everyday life on the Pine Ridge Reservation.

2015 Plans are made to discuss the fate of the Black Hills with President Barack Obama.

GLOSSARY

counting coup Touching an enemy in battle to prove one's bravery.

cradleboard A wooden board used to carry a baby.

Dakota A Siouan word meaning "friend." Also, the language spoken by the Santee Sioux.

Ghost Dance A religion that swept across the tribes of the Great Plains in the late 1800s.

homestead To acquire land and farm it for a period of time before it becomes officially owned.

howitzer A cannon.

Lakota A Siouan language spoken by the Teton Sioux. Also the name of the Tetons.

moccasin A soft leather shoe often decorated with colorful beads or quills.

nomadic Moving seasonally from one place to another.

Paha Sapa The Sioux name for the sacred Black Hills of South Dakota.

pemmican Pounded dry meat mixed with fat and berries used as "energy food" when warriors went on long journeys.

quillwork Decorative embroidery patterns created with the quills of porcupines or birds.

reservation An area of land on which a Native American community lives.

sedentary Kept in one place.

sovereignty The right and ability of a people to govern themselves and their nation.

Sun Dance The most important Sioux ceremony, held each summer.

sweat lodge A dome-shaped hut covered with bison skins in which purifications and other sacred ceremonies are held.

tiyospaye A group of families belonging to the same Sioux band.

travois A sled made of two poles lashed together and pulled by a dog or horse.

vision quest A coming-of-age ceremony of solitary fasting for four days to induce dreams in young people.

Wakan Tanka The Great Spirit who watches over all living things.

warbonnet A feathered headdress worn by great Sioux warriors.

BIBLIOGRAPHY

Anderson, Gary C. *Through Dakota Eyes: Narrative Accounts of the Minnesota Indian War of 1862.* St. Paul, MN: Minnesota Historical Society Press, 1988.

Berg, Scott W. *38 Nooses: Lincoln, Little Crow, and the Beginning of the Frontier's End.* New York: Vintage Books, 2012.

Bowman, Donna Janell. *The Sioux: The Past and Present of the Dakota, Lakota, and Nakota.* American Indian Life. North Mankato, MN: Capstone Press, 2015.

Brown, Dee. *Bury My Heart at Wounded Knee: An Indian History of the American West.* New York: Owl Books, 1970.

Cunningham, Kevin, and Peter Benoit. *The Sioux.* True Books. New York: Scholastic, 2011.

Drury, Bob, and Tom Clavin. *The Heart of Everything That Is: The Untold Story of Red Cloud, An American Legend.* New York: Simon & Schuster, 2013.

Marshall, Joseph M. III. *The Journey of Crazy Horse.* New York: Biking, 2004.

Michno, Gregory F. *Dakota Dawn: The Decisive First Week of the Sioux Uprising, August 17–24, 1862.* El Dorado Hills, CA: Savas Beatie, 2011.

Neilhardt, John G. *Black Elk Speaks.* Albany, NY: State University of New York Press, 2008.

Nelson, S.D. *Sitting Bull: Lakota Warrior and Defender of His People.* New York: Abrams Books for Young Readers, 2015.

Philbrick, Nathaniel. *The Last Stand: Custer, Sitting Bull, and the Battle of Little Bighorn.* New York: Viking, 2011.

Powers, Thomas. *The Killing of Crazy Horse.* New York: Vintage Books, 2010.

Teicher, Jordan G. "A Photographer's Moving Tribute to the Pine Ridge Reservation." Slate. February 20, 2014. Accessed November 13, 2015. http://www.slate.com/blogs/behold/2014/02/20/aaron_huey_photographs_the_pine_ridge_reservation_in_south_dakota_in_his.html.

Utley, Robert M. *Sitting Bull: The Life and Times of an American Patriot.* New York: Henry Holt and Company, 2008.

Zimmerman, Dwight Jon. *Saga of the Sioux: An Adaptation of Dee Brown's Bury My Heart at Wounded Knee.* New York: Henry Holt and Company, 2014.

FURTHER INFORMATION

Want to know more about the Sioux? Check out these websites, videos, and organizations.

Websites

Crazy Horse Memorial

crazyhorsememorial.org

Learn about the people and ongoing plans behind the building of a memorial dedicated to Crazy Horse.

History: Sitting Bull

www.history.com/topics/native-american-history/sitting-bull

This website presents articles and videos about the history of Sitting Bull, a renowned Sioux leader.

Video

Crash Course US History: Westward Expansion

www.youtube.com/watch?v=Q16OZkgSXfM

This video, presented by best-selling author John Green, discusses the conditions of the American West in the 1800s.

Organizations

Akta Lakota Museum and Cultural Center

St Joseph's Indian School

PO Box 89

Chamberlain, SD 57325

(800) 798-3452

aktalakota.stjo.org

Cheyenne River Sioux Tribe

PO Box 590

Eagle Butte, SD 57625

(605) 964-4155

www.sioux.org

Crow Creek Sioux Tribe

PO Box 50

Fort Thompson, SD 57339

(605) 245-2221

www.crowcreekconnections.org

Flandreau Santee Sioux Tribe

Flandreau Field Office

PO Box 283

Flandreau, SD 57028

(605) 997-3891

www.santeesioux.com

Lower Brule Sioux Tribe

PO Box 187

Lower Brule, SD 57548

(605) 473-5561

www.lbst.org

Lower Sioux Indian Community

32469 Redwood County Hwy

Morton, MN 56270

(507) 697-6321

www.lowersioux.com

Oglala Sioux Tribe

PO Box 2070

Pine Ridge, SD 57770

(605) 867-8468

www.oglalalakotanation.org

Red Cloud Indian School

100 Mission Drive, Pine Ridge Indian Reservation

Pine Ridge, SD 57770

(605) 867-1105

www.redcloudschool.org

Rosebud Sioux Tribe

11 Legion Avenue

Rosebud, SD 57570

(888) 747-2381

www.rosebudsiouxtribe-nsn.gov

Santee Sioux Nation

108 Spirit Lake Avenue West

Niobrara, NE 68760

(402) 857-2772

www.santeesiouxnation.net

Shakopee Mdewakanton Sioux Community

2330 Sioux Trail NW

Prior Lake, MN 55372

(952) 445-8900

www.shakopeedakota.org

Sisseton Wahpeton Oyate of The Lake Traverse Reservation

PO Box 509

Agency Village, SD 57262

(605) 698-3911

www.swo-nsn.gov

Standing Rock Sioux Tribe

Building #1 Standing Rock Avenue

PO Box D

Fort Yates, ND 58538

(701) 854-8500

standingrock.org

Upper Sioux Community

5722 Travers Lane

PO Box 147

Granite Falls, MN 56241

(320) 564-3853

www.uppersiouxcommunity-nsn.gov

Yankton Sioux Tribe

PO Box 1153

Wagner, SD 57380

(605) 384-3641

www.yanktonsiouxtribe.net

INDEX

ABOUT THE AUTHORS

Cassie M. Lawton is a freelance editor and writer living and working in New York City.

Raymond Bial has published more than eighty books—most of them photography books—during his career. His photo-essays for children include *Corn Belt Harvest, Amish Home, Frontier Home, Shaker Home, The Underground Railroad, Portrait of a Farm Family, With Needle and Thread: A Book About Quilts, Mist Over the Mountains: Appalachia and Its People, Cajun Home,* and *Where Lincoln Walked.*

As with his other work, Bial's deep feeling for his subjects is evident in both the text and illustrations. He travels to tribal cultural centers, photographing homes, artifacts, and surroundings and learning firsthand about the national lifeways of these peoples.

The emeritus director of a small college library in the Midwest, he lives with his wife and three children in Urbana, Illinois.